---

# FREE BOOKS

## *www.forgottenbooks.org*

---

You can read literally <u>thousands</u> of books
for free at www.forgottenbooks.org

*(please support us by visiting our web site)*

Truth may seem, but cannot be:
Beauty brag, but 'tis not she;
Truth and beauty buried be.

To this urn let those repair
That are either true or fair;
For these dead birds sigh a prayer.

**Bacon**

# JOHNS HOPKINS UNIVERSITY STUDIES

IN

# HISTORICAL AND POLITICAL SCIENCE

———————

## EXTRA VOLUME
## XXIV

# HISTORY OF SLAVERY

IN

# VIRGINIA

BY

## JAMES CURTIS BALLAGH

*Associate in History, Johns Hopkins University*

———

BALTIMORE
THE JOHNS HOPKINS PRESS
1902

JOHN MURPHY COMPANY, PRINTERS,

BALTIMORE.

TO THE MEMORY OF

MY AUNTS

SUSAN CATHERINE WITHROW

AND

PHOEBE CAROLINE PATTERSON

# CONTENTS.

                                                      PAGE

PREFACE................................................................................. vii

CHAPTER I.  SLAVE TRADE AND SLAVE POPULATION.

    Slavery as a Stage in Social Progress....................... 1
    Origin and Progress of the Modern Slave Trade............... 3
    Importation of the Subjects of Slavery..................... 6
    Restrictive Duties and Petitions to the Crown.................... 11
    Prohibition Attempted and Realized........................... 19
    Slave Population and the Domestic Slave Trade............... 24

CHAPTER II.  DEVELOPMENT OF SLAVERY.

*Legal Status of the Slave.*

    Origin of Status........................................... 27
    Status of the Early Negroes and Indians..................... 28
    Relation of Servitude to Slavery........................... 31
    Subjects and Principles of Enslavement....................... 45
    Mulattoes, Mestizos and Persons of Color.................... 56
    Incidents of Slavery; Rights and Duties..................... 62
    Penal Legislation concerning Slaves........................ 82

*Social Status of the Slave.*

    Regulation by Custom....................................... 96
    Personality of the Slave and Customary Rights.............. 97
    Maintenance, Guardianship, Education and Liberty.......... 102
    Negro Preachers........................................... 110

CHAPTER III.  MANUMISSION, EMANCIPATION AND THE FREE MAN.

    Withdrawal of Restrictions to Liberty...................... 116
    Public and Private Manumission............................ 119
    Suits for Freedom......................................... 123
    Transportation of Freedmen................................ 125
    Anti-Slavery Sentiment.................................... 127
    Plans for Emancipation.................................... 130
    Slavery Polemics and Apologetics.......................... 142
    Status of the Free Negro.................................. 145

BIBLIOGRAPHY............................................................ 149

# PREFACE.

In the literature upon American slavery there is no such distinctive study of its institutional origin, development and relations as has been made of certain similar forms of social organization in Europe. This fact will serve to explain the method, constructive rather than narrative, of the present volume and the reference, somewhat more general than the title suggests, to the experience of other American colonies and States, and to that of Europe where it has seemed necessary.

It is recognized that objective views of the local character of slavery in every division of the present United States where it has existed are prerequisite to its true history in this country. My wish has been to contribute to this end by a careful investigation of the institution as it existed in one of these, Virginia, with a candid statement of results. The priority of this colony and the long coexistence there of forms of dependence give unusual interest and value to its institutional experience, and make it the natural starting point of the general inquiry.

For the invariable kindness with which the historical materials relating to the subject have been made accessible to me I desire to thank particularly, among many who have aided me, Messrs. Philip A. Bruce and W. G. Stanard, of the Virginia Historical Society; W. W. Scott, of the Virginia State Library; John L. Campbell, Secretary of the Washington and Lee University; Frederick W. Page, Librarian of the University of Virginia; Dr. Philip R. Uhler, Provost of the Peabody Library, Baltimore, and Hon. A. R. Spofford, of the Library of Congress, Washington.

Portions of Chapter II. have appeared, in somewhat modified form, in the pages of the *Conservative Review* and the permission to make use of this matter is due to the courtesy of the editors of that periodical.

I take especial pleasure in acknowledging my indebtedness to my colleagues, Professor J. M. Vincent for valuable assistance at every stage of the progress of the book through the press, and Professor W. W. Willoughby who also has read the proof-sheets, and to Mr. N. Murray, of the Johns Hopkins Press, for suggestions.

Acknowledgment due to others is to be found in the footnotes and in the appended bibliography.

J. C. B.

JOHNS HOPKINS UNIVERSITY,
*April 8,* 1902.

# HISTORY OF SLAVERY IN VIRGINIA.

## CHAPTER I.

### THE SLAVE TRADE AND SLAVE POPULATION.

African slavery has had a long institutional history. Both the literature and the monuments of ancient Egypt show that the Ethiopian slave was known not only to classical but to remote antiquity. The origin of domestic slavery in Africa is to be referred to the same general cause to which are ascribed other historic forms of slavery, viz.: some essential or actual inequality between individuals or sets of individuals in their broad social relations. Such an inequality continued and intensified, gradually and almost imperceptibly creates a status marked by distinct incidents, which in time assumes the form of a definite social institution, recognized first in custom, then in law.

Slavery represents thus a stage in social progress, tending constantly to emerge wherever social units of unlike order or capacity are brought into continued competitive contact in the struggle for existence. The practical economic and political principle of subordination in such a case replaces the more theoretical conception of coördination and coöperation. Historically speaking, industrial society in a large sense has, without exception, been founded upon the subserviency of one activity or agent of labor, or set of such activities or agents, to another. The gradation of labor forms, even in the case of a single individual agent, is but the simplest expression of a similar truth. As society is not composed of a single unit, neither is it composed, as at present constituted, of compound

1

equal ones. Society, and particularly industrial society, is essentially complex. Complexity appears within the simplest social unit itself, and is reflected in the *manus* of the husband and in the *dominium* of the father, which latter in ancient society developed institutionally into the *patria potestas.* The Roman *clientela* and the German *comitatus* illustrate the same truth, more especially in the political sphere. Ancient slavery, mediæval vassalage and villainage, modern servitude and slavery, and forms of dependent so-called free labor all partake of a common quality of subordination in their origin and development. From a past institutional standpoint at least the mere existence of such results sufficiently denies the doctrine of natural equality and inalienable rights in the social sphere. Given inequality of capacity or condition, whether natural or acquired, the evolution of the various forms in which dependent labor has found expression is determined by environment, and the particular form by the degree of the relation of dependence.

Historic connection then of examples of these various forms as antecedent and consequent is not a necessary assumption, though in some cases it is a certain or plausible one. In the case of slavery at least the various phases it assumed in ancient times, in Babylonia, Egypt, Assyria, Phoenicia, Greece and Rome for instance, present an institutional continuity that may have been based more or less upon actual contact, but it is also true that local conditions have existed amongst all known peoples at some stage of their development sufficient to account for the native origin of the most characteristic features of this institution. We may assume, then, in the absence of evidence to the contrary, that African slavery had such an independent origin and that in development its connection with past as with future foreign forms of slavery was one of institutional similarity rather than of causal relation. Regardless of the continuity of the idea of modern slavery in Africa, Europe, and America, it is to be remembered that the sanction and growth of slavery depended upon local causes, and for this reason its form and incidents materially differed in these three countries and indeed in different parts of the same country. Thus the patriarchal institution of the English colonies had little in common with the type of the penal or galley slave to be found in the Spanish West Indies.

The era of awakened commerce and discovery, that marked the transition of the mediæval into the modern world, first brought Europeans into contact with African slavery as an already developed institution. Negroes under their tribal customs enslaved their kindred for debt, for crime, and as a matter of systematic poor relief. So, too, the sparing of the captive enemy to become a slave, the most fertile and humane source of slavery, was commonly practiced in native inter-tribal warfare.[1] The Moors, also, from early times enslaved not only the blacks around them but also Christian whites.[2] It was through the Moors that Europeans were first made acquainted with the benefits to be derived from the African slave trade.

When in the first half of the fifteenth century,[3] the energetic Prince Henry of Portugal, better known as Prince Henry the Navigator, was actively pushing the course of Portuguese discovery along the west coast of Africa, Antony Gonzales, one of his mariners, captured, in 1440, two Moors near Cape Bajados. The prince ordered the exchange of the Moors for a proffered ransom of ten blacks, and these were brought from the Rio del Oro to Lisbon in 1442. He justified his act on the ground that the negroes might be Christianized but the Moors could not. Two years later the Company of Lagos, chartered by the king and engaged in discovery on the African coast, imported two hundred negroes from the islands of Nar and Tidar. Of these the king received his

---

[1] Snelgrave, *Account of Guinea*, 158.
[2] Helps, *Spanish Conquest in America*, I., 30.
[3] Helps, *ibid.*, I., 19, *et seq.*; Brock, *Va. Hist. Soc. Coll.*, VI., 2. This was between the years 1419 and 1463.

share, a fifth.   They were parted by lot irrespective of rela-
tionship, justification for the subjection of their bodies being
found in a pious hope for the salvation of their souls.[4]

Such was the beginning of the African slave trade in
Europe, an incident of the commercial expansion of Portugal, an accident in the general progress of the world to en-
lightenment, and on the very eve of the birth of a new era.
Within a few years thirty-seven Portuguese ships were engaged in the trade, and in 1481 the king felt constrained to
add to his distinctions the title "Lord of Guinea."   After
the discovery of America and the colonization of the Spanish
West Indies, the inefficiency of Indian slave labor in the
mines, and the questionable humanity of Las Casas, led to the
substitution of negro labor.   Thus at the beginning of the
sixteenth century, 1502 and 1503, a field was opened for the
slave trade that even Portugal could not fill.[5]   The traffic
was consequently undertaken by Spain in 1517, and by the
English Hawkins in 1553.[6]   France followed in 1624, and
somewhat later Holland, Denmark, New England and other
English colonies.   All civilized nations with any extended
commerce were engaged in the trade.   Slaves were sold into
Portugal, Spain, and England, but particularly into the
American colonies—continental and island—of Spain, France,
England, Portugal and Holland.   The main supply was
directed to the Spanish West Indies, in early days quite
naturally from their prior discovery and settlement, and in
later days because importation was found to be cheaper than
the breeding of slaves.

The leader in the trade and the last to abandon it was
Great Britain, though she did not regularly enter it until

---

[4] Helps, *idem*, I., 30–32, 35–40.

[5] Brock, *Va. Hist. Soc. Coll.*, VI., 2; Edwards, *West Indies*, II., cap. 15;
cf. *ibid.*, II., 239; Herrera, *Historia General*, I., d. 5, c. 12.

[6] Edwards, *ibid.*, II., 240, 241; cf. Hakluyt, quoted by Cobb, *Slavery*, cxiii,
in Brock, *ibid.*, VI., 2.

comparatively late. Queen Elizabeth is said to have been a partner of Hawkins in several voyages, and to have issued a patent for the traffic in the 30th year of her reign. It is not certain, however, that any voyage was made under her patent.[7] The first attempt by England to establish a systematic trade was made November 16, 1618, when a patent was granted to Sir Robert Rich, later Earl of Warwick, and others to form a company for the purpose. Ships were fitted out, but the profits of the trade not answering expectations the charter was suffered to lapse. A second African Company was chartered by Charles I. in 1631, and a third and exclusive Company was formed in 1633, which enjoyed a large trade for a quarter of a century until the abolition of monopolies under William and Mary opened the trade to the whole nation.[8] A fourth charter was granted in 1670. Between 1712 and 1749, according to the stipulations of the treaty of Utrecht, the exclusive privilege of supplying slaves to the Spanish colonies was granted to the English South Sea Company by Spain, half of the stock of the company being held by the British queen and the Spanish king, and the operations of the African Company and private adventurers were limited to the British colonies. In 1749 the whole field of the trade was thrown open to Englishmen. It was probably at its height just before the war of the American Revolution, when Great Britain had 192 ships employed, and transported 47,000 negroes annually to the colonies. Of the 6,000,000 to 9,000,000 slaves imported up to this time, British subjects are said to have carried half. No small portion was carried by colonial ships, which had been engaged in the traffic since 1646.[9]

---

[7] Dabney, *Defense of Virginia and the South*, 27; Census 1860, Population, XIV.

[8] Dabney, *ibid.*, 27; cf. Edwards, *West Indies*, 247, *n.*

[9] Edwards, *ibid.*, II., 260; Dabney, *ibid.*, 28, 29; Census 1860, Population, XIV. London, Liverpool, and Bristol, England; and Boston and Bristol, New England, were the chief centres of the trade, but Charleston, Baltimore

The island colonies of England lying in the path of West India commerce were naturally the first of her foreign possessions to receive importations of Africans, and during the seventeenth century they were the chief regions outside of the Spanish West Indies supplied by the slavers. For institutional beginnings of the system of American negro slavery we are to look, then, to the Bermudas and to Barbadoes rather than to Virginia, Massachusetts, or New York. How far the rules regulating the relation of master and slave in the Spanish colonies influenced the custom and legislation of the English is difficult to determine. The contrast in the two resulting slave systems, if it be a safe guide, suggests that if any influence existed between them it was extremely meagre. Some connection, however, is shown between the systems of the island and mainland colonies of England, particularly in the influence of the Bermudas upon South Carolina.

The introduction of the negro as a profitable labor supply in the English as in the Spanish colonies was the result of a deliberate commercial design. A London mercantile company, the "Company for the Summers Islands," sent in 1616 one of its trading ships to the West Indies for products, such as sugar cane, which it hoped to introduce into the Bermudas, and for "negroes to dive for pearles." The first negro, together with a single Indian, and West Indian products, were brought back late in the summer of that year. The relation of the negro to the profitable cultivation of sugar cane was soon discovered and fresh importations were made.[10] In

---

and Norfolk were participants. In 1806, two years before the trade was made illicit, 74,000 negroes were being imported into the West Indies alone. Britain led in the trade, France was second, Portugal third, the Dutch next with 4,000, and the Danes fifth with 2,000.

[10] Lefroy, *Memorials of Bermuda*, I., 115. In the instructions to Daniel Tucker, first Governor of Bermuda under the company (he got his commission February 15, 1615), the order for sending out such a ship under Mr. Wilmott is mentioned. Late in the summer of 1616 (cf. Lefroy, *History of Bermudas*, 84, 85, 99, and Brown, *Genesis of the United States*, 824),

April, 1618, Sir Robert Rich, a prominent member of this company for the Summers Islands and of the Virginia Company, in connection with Deputy Governor Argall, of Virginia, and other associates sent a ship under an old commission of the Duke of Savoy, Charles Emmanuel I., to rove in West Indian waters and to prey upon Spanish commerce.[11] This ship Argall in his private capacity as part owner, fitted out in Virginia ostensibly for trade with the Indians on the coast and among the islands for skins and goats, though his real object was piracy upon Spanish commerce.[12]  On its course to the West Indies the *Treasurer* touched at the Bermudas, and Deputy Governor Kendall, contrary to the order and advice of Governor Tucker (who was just leaving for England and feared diplomatic complications with Spain), received the ship ostensibly as the Earl of Warwick's.  He even provided it with provisions and other necessaries from the public store, on condition of being admitted to a share of its plunder as a rover, a fact which was now candidly admitted.  The result of its voyage was a cargo of negroes, with which it returned to Virginia in the fall of 1619. Yeardley having succeeded Argall in the government and the Virginians being afraid of trouble with Spain, the *Treasurer*

---

the ship *Edwin*, belonging to the company (commanded in 1618 and 1619 by Capt. Bargrave), which had been on a similar errand, came into the Bermudas bringing with the products "one Indian and one negro, the first to arrive."

[11] This was the famous *Treasurer*, which had rendered service for many years in the settlement of Virginia as a transport ship for the Virginia Company, and in voyages along the American coast for discovery, supplies, and acts of hostility against French and Dutch settlements.  The commission had been issued in 1616 for English aid in the war between Savoy and Spain.  Brown, *Genesis of the United States*, 980.

[12] Lefroy, *Bermudas*, I., 133, 134, 147, 148; cf. Neil, *Virginia Carolorum*, 34; Burk, *Virginia*, I., 319; Smith (Arber), same account in brief, 667 (or in other editions, 190); Purchas, *His Pilgrims*, 1734, 1764, 1774, 1798, 1804; Massachusetts Historical Collections, 4th S., IX., 4 n.; *Virginia Company Records*, I., 73; II., 197, 202.

and its mission were thoroughly discountenanced by the colony. The rover therefore sailed away secretly for the Bermudas after landing at Jamestown a single negro, and that one, probably, because she was a woman. The remainder of the cargo, twenty-nine negroes, were taken to the Bermudas early in September, 1619.[13] Shortly before this a Dutch frigate, manned chiefly with English, a consort of the *Treasurer*, and pretending to sail under a commission of the Duke of Orange, but actually uncommissioned and hence a "pirate," had presented Governor Kendall of the Bermudas with fourteen negroes, and other plunder captured in the West Indies, in exchange for provisions and munitions. The exchange was made on the understanding that Kendall was to share in the results of its further depredations. This ship, before coming to the Bermudas, had touched at Jamestown "about the last of August," 1619, and sold the colonists twenty negroes.[14] These were the first negroes introduced into the

---

[13] Hotten, *Immigrants*, 224; Brown, *Genesis*, 886.

[14] Smith, *Works* (Arber), 541; Lefroy, *Bermudas*, 144, 145, 155; Brown, *Genesis*, 968, 980; Massachusetts Historical Society Collections, IX., 5. This matter has been considered at greater length than the subject seems to justify, as much misapprehension, involving misstatement and controversy, has arisen from attempts to place upon one nation or the other responsibility for the introduction of the first negro "slaves" into North America. The Rev. Edward D. Neil in his *Virginia Vetusta*, and *Virginia Carolorum*, and other writings on Virginia history, first tried to establish the fact, in direct opposition to the statements of contemporaries, Rolfe and Secretary John Pory, that the *Treasurer*, "a Virginia ship," and not a Dutch ship, brought the first twenty negroes to Virginia. Mr. Alexander Brown in his *Genesis of the United States* (885, 980) concurs in Neil's opinion. Mr. Philip Bruce, the economic historian of early Virginia, in an able discussion of several pages, effectually clears the London Company and the *Treasurer* from any responsibility as to the introduction of the first twenty negroes, concurring with Stith, Beverley (51), Burk (I., 211), Campbell (144, 528), and Bancroft in an endorsement of Rolfe's statement that they were brought in by a Dutch ship. He appears to me, however, to be in error in endorsing Neil's statement that the Dutch vessel touched at the Bermudas *en route* to Virginia ( *Virginia Vetusta*, 113; *Economic History of Virginia*, II., 67), and also to confuse the negroes brought by that ship (Kerbye's

colony of Virginia. In the next four years there seems to have been little importation of negroes into either Virginia or the Bermudas. English trading ships on their way from the West Indies brought these no doubt more by accident than by design. Thus the *James* in 1621, the *Margaret and John* in 1622, and the *Swan* in 1623 each brought a single negro into Virginia. In 1625, more than five years after the first introduction of negroes into Virginia, when the white population was about 2,500, there were but twenty-three negroes in the colony, the same number as in 1623, one child having been born and one negro having died; so for more than two years no importation seems to have been made.

Importation remained of this occasional nature well through the first half of the seventeenth century. Thirty years after the first introduction of negroes only 300 were to be found in

---

frigate) to the Bermudas with those landed by the *Treasurer* subsequently. Stith (143, 153; cf. *Colonial Records of Virginia*, pp. 76, 77) thinks Lord Delaware was partial owner of the *Treasurer*, and tries to cloak Argall for manning and victualling her under Delaware's orders. He is probably guilty of anachronism. Beverly and Burk mistake the date as 1620 instead of 1619, and Williams, the negro historian of his race, puts it in 1618 (*History of the Negro Race*, I., 117). The latter makes some unfortunate mistakes, confusing the Governor of Bermudas with the Governor of Virginia (*Idem*, I., 118); the fourteen negroes of the Bermudas with the twenty of Virginia; and he suggests that Smith (*i. e.*, Rolfe) meant to say something very different from what he did say,—that when he said the negroes were sold by a Dutch man-of-war "about the last of August," 1619, he intended to say "about the end of last August" (*Idem*, I., 116; Smith, II., 37). To make assurance doubly sure he contradicts himself by saying that the *Treasurer* brought the first negroes in 1618, but the Dutch ship landed her cargo in 1619. Yet he correctly identifies the Dutch ship with the "pirate frigate" of Kirbye. This is a fair illustration of what confusion a very small matter can occasion. The statements of the authorities, Rolfe and Pory, the records of the Virginia Company, and Smith in his *History of Virginia*, and again in his *Bermudas* (if he be the author of the MSS. edited by Lefroy), are difficult to reconcile fully, particularly as the dates are given in general terms and not explicitly, and as the matter came into controversy in 1623. Smith's account seems to show partisanship for Warwick, that of the Virginia Company for Kendall (see I., 540).

Virginia, a number of whom were no doubt the result of natural increase.   But by 1659 the value of negro labor even amongst the preponderating white servants was beginning to be realized, and the assembly legislated in favor of its importation.   The allowance of a head right for the negro after 1635 as for any other immigrant, and the scarcity of labor in the rapid colonial expansion, account for the rise of the new demand.   Some Virginia planters obtained large estates through head rights for imported negroes and whites.   These facts also help to explain the enslavement of the negro which followed in 1661, and the formation by Englishmen of a third and exclusive company for the slave trade in 1662.

It is to the operations of this company and to individual English traders that Virginia was indebted for the most of her slaves.   From 1664 to 1671 several shiploads of negroes were brought in, but servants continued to be imported at the greater rate of 1,500 a year, and in 1671 there were 6,000 servants to 2,000 slaves in Virginia.[15]   By 1683 the number of servants had doubled, while that of the slaves had increased by only one third.[16]   From this time forth servitude gave way before slavery, which was forced on the colony in the large importation of negroes by the Royal African Company under its exclusive charter.   It was the policy of the king, and of the Duke of York, who stood at the head of the Company, to hasten the adoption of slavery by enactments cutting off the supply of indented servants, at the same time that large importations of slaves were made by their agents.   The laws of 1676 and 1682 which legalized Indian slavery coöperated still further to increase the slave population.   In 1698 the African trade was thrown open to separate traders.   An active competition at once sprang up with the African Com-

---

[15] Hening, *Statutes at Large*, II., 515; Force, *Tracts*, III., VIII.; Bruce, *Economic History of Virginia*, II., 75, 76, 78.

[16] Doyle, *Virginia et cet.*, 383.

pany, the separate traders importing large numbers of negroes and attempting to undersell the Company.

With these importations the colonists seemed to realize the dangers involved in African slavery. Though in 1659 they had given practical encouragement to the importation of negroes by the Dutch, they now felt constrained to discourage the increase of a dangerous population by subjecting negroes and alien servants to discriminating duties.[17] Such a duty was laid by an act of 1699 for three years and was continued in 1701. That this was not purely a revenue act is shown by the fact that a rebate of three-fourths of the duty was given when the negroes were transported out of the Dominion within six weeks. The duty was continued by the acts of 1704 and 1705, in which it was laid simply upon " negroes or other slaves." The excuse of revenue, it is true, was alleged and brief time limitations were given to the acts, but these limitations were designed to procure England's confirmation of the enactments. When large and successive increases were made, the slave traders readily saw that the intent was to lay prohibitive duties. They consequently protested vigorously, and secured the withholding of the king's assent to as many as thirty-three different acts passed by the Virginia Assembly prior to 1772 to discourage the slave trade.[18]

The importation of negroes remained practically unchecked, however, and the only advantage Virginia reaped from such of these acts as became laws was a large revenue for her public works. In 1705 negroes to the number of 1,800 were brought in, and in 1708 there were in the colony 12,000 negro tithables as compared with 18,000 white. Projected insurrections of negroes in 1710, 1722, and 1730 bear witness to their alarming increase, and by the middle of the century

---

[17] Hening, III., 193.   Negroes were taxed 20 s. and alien servants 15 s. a head.

[18] Hening, I., 540; III., 193, 213, 225, 229, 233; Tucker, *Blackstone*, I., 51, append.

the blacks were almost as numerous as the whites. The stipulations of the treaty of Utrecht which excluded the operations of the English traders from the Spanish-American colonies between 1712 and 1749 were largely responsible for the rapid increase of negroes in the English colonies.[19] In 1715 there were 23,000 negroes in a white population of 72,500 in Virginia, and by 1756 the negroes numbered 120,156 and the whites but 173,316. Thirty-eight of the forty-nine counties had more negro than white tithables, and eleven of the counties had a negro population varying from one-fourth to one-half more than the white. In twenty counties the white and the black populations were nearly equal. It was only in the new counties on the frontier that negroes were so few[20] as not to cause serious alarm.

Regardless of increasing duties, the large shipments of the African Company and of traders in England and the colonies continued. The main centres of the traffic in England were London, Bristol, and Liverpool; in New England, Boston and Bristol, and in the South, Charleston, South Carolina. In 1726 the three English cities alone had 171 ships engaged in the trade, and its profits were said to warrant the employment of a thousand more, though such a number was probably never reached as far as England alone was concerned. From 1804 to 1807 Great Britain had 70 ships in the trade; Charleston, South Carolina, 61; Rhode Island, 59; Baltimore, 4; Norfolk, 2; and Boston 1.

But the "separate" traders were making the largest importations. They sent 50,000 annually to all the colonies, while the African Company sent but 5,400, and for several years fewer of these had come to Virginia than to North Carolina and Maryland. In fact, Virginia was so well supplied with negroes at this time that although the profits of

---

[19] *Virginia MSS., B. R. O.,* V. pt. 2, p. 352; II., pt. 1., 211; *ibid.,* November 27, 1708; *Calendar Virginia State Papers,* I., 129, 130.
    [20] *Dinwiddie Papers,* II., 345, 474.

their labor were greater than in some colonies there seems to have been a temporary falling off in a supply[21] that had tended constantly to increase since the shipments of the African Company had begun. In 1676 the Company had sent 650 negroes to Virginia, who were sold at an average of £18 a head.[22] The price rose rapidly with enlarged demand. Regardless of the fact that Governor Nicholson, with the approval of the Lords of Trade, had in 1699 discontinued the land grants given for importation, prices reached a maximum of £28 and £35 a head in the following year. There were actually as many buyers, it was said, as negroes offered for sale. The Governor thought that even 2,000 negroes would meet with ready sale, and the traders redoubled their efforts at the very time that the more thoughtful colonists, now beginning to realize the dangers of an African population, were attempting to restrict importations. From 1710 to 1718, notwithstanding the fact that a duty of £5 a head was exacted, importation was not effectively checked and the revenue collections from slaves amounted to $15,000. By 1723 negroes were coming at the rate of 1,500 or 1,600 a year.[23] This number was still further increased during the succeeding years in which a duty was not laid or was ineffective through repeals of the colonial revenue acts in England.

In 1723, for the first time, the English slave traders in general seemed to awake to the real intent of the Virginia Assembly in the professed revenue duties laid upon liquors and slaves. The enlarged trade that they had enjoyed since the expiration of the £5 duty in 1718 showed them the loss they might expect to sustain with a renewed duty. They made a combined effort, consequently, for the repeal of a law

---

[21] *Virginia MSS., B. R. O.*, 1726, April 2. In North Carolina negroes were coming at the rate of 1,000 a year and many brought better prices than in Virginia and Maryland. DeBow, *Resources of the South,* I., 341.

[22] *Calendar of English State Papers*, Colonial, 444, 552.

[23] *Virginia MSS., B. R. O.*, II., pt. 1, 111, 211, 297, January 17, 1723.

passed by the Assembly in 1723, though the duty laid was but 40 s. which was less than half the former duty. They were fortunate in being able to attack the law on technical as well as on commercial grounds, and the complete success of this first attempt encouraged repeated efforts, most of which were effective, against succeeding laws of a similar nature that the Assembly was brave enough to pass.

In this legislation, as well as in the candid statements of representative Virginians, we find most conclusive proofs of the early hostile attitude of the colonists toward a negro population, as well as of their powerlessness to shape their economic and social development where it conflicted with the general plan of English commercial policy. No colony made a more strenuous and prolonged effort to prevent the imposition of negro slavery upon it, and no State a more earnest attempt to alleviate or rid itself of that burden than Virginia. Both efforts failed from inexorable political and economic conditions over which the Virginians had but little control. The sincerity of their desire is, however, evinced from the extreme measures resorted to to gain their end. The colonists justified themselves, in view of the unjust methods of the Mother Country, in employing the arts of diplomatic deception, and political pressure, whenever emergencies arose that gave them an advantage. When such means failed they resorted to humble pleading, and finally to outspoken condemnation of the English policy and to threatened rebellion.

By skilful wording of preambles and brief limitations to the acts imposing duties, and by judicious expenditure upon public works of the revenue raised, the colonists had partially concealed the true intent of the acts during the first ten years. The Assembly of 1710 became bolder, and, pressed by the exigencies of the growing over-production and low prices of tobacco and by the general indebtedness for the increasing purchases of negroes, advanced the duty on negro slaves to £5, while it left the tariff on liquors and on Indians as before. Governor Spotswood was not slow to see that the design was to discourage the impórtation of negro slaves, and he remonstrated with the members of the Assembly, urging them to abandon the bill or to lower the duty. The arguments of the colonists, however, were unanswerable, and the Assembly finally refused to yield. As Spotswood was unwilling to oppose "the general inclination of the country" he allowed the act to pass and made such apologies to the authorities in England as he hoped would prevent opposition from the slave traders. He alleged that the planters were practically bankrupt and could not or would not purchase any slaves until the price of tobacco improved, which was not reasonably to be expected within the three years limitation of the act.[24]

---

[24] *Spotswood Letters*, I., 52; Hening, III., 482. Previous to this, five acts laying duties are extant. The act of 1699 imposed a duty of 5 s. more upon slaves than servants, and provision for strict enforcement was made under heavy penalty. The necessity of replacing the Statehouse of the colony, lately destroyed by fire, and the desire to avoid an extra poll tax was the excuse alleged. If revenue had been the sole object, however, English and not alien servants, who were few in number, would have been included in the act. Its limitation was three years, but before expiration in 1701 it was continued to December 25, 1703, and a drawback of three-fourths of the duty was allowed on slaves transported out of the colony within six weeks. A committee for the fifth revisal of the laws had been appointed in 1699, and it was expected that they would report before the expiration of this act. The report was delayed, however, until 1705, so that in April, 1704, an act for one year had to be passed reviving the duty, which had not been collected for the four months intervening. In September, 1704, the Council of Virginia imposed an extra duty of 2 s. per slave for the alleged purpose of rebuilding William and Mary College, which had been burned. The revisal of 1705 continued the duty for two years, taking precaution to include all slaves sent in from North Carolina and Maryland, by which means importers had begun to evade duties. This act probably expired by limitation May 25, 1707, after raising a revenue of £4,000, of which £3,000 was expended in building a governor's house. No Acts of Assembly between 1706 and 1710 are extant, so that it is impossible to say whether the duty was continued or not. But a special revenue act for the support of the government, laying a duty of 6 s. per poll on all servants and 'slaves imported, was in effect from 1705 to June 22, 1708, when it was repealed by proclamation. In 1710 this act was also revived.

This high duty was continued by two other acts, 1712 and 1714, until the year 1718. Spotswood allowed these also to pass. He explained that they were necessary to keep up public credit and to pay the debts "already contracted;" but it is evident that his statement was made in fear that their provisions might prove disagreeable to England.[25] It was quickly shown that his fear was well grounded, but the objections raised in England were not serious enough to withstand the arguments of Spotswood backed by the actual benefits the colony could show for her judicious expenditure of the large revenue raised.[26] From 1718 until 1723, for some reason that does not fully appear, a duty was not collected. It would seem from a remark of Thomas Jefferson's that the Assembly was either careless or was influenced by some peculiar circumstance—probably pressure from England— that demanded the repeal of the duty. At any rate, this "inconsiderate" action, as Jefferson termed it, met with a "joyful sanction" from the English Crown, which from that time forth resented all attempts to renew a duty.[27] A duty of 40 s. laid by the act of May, 1723, was effective until October 27, 1724, when it was repealed by royal proclamation. The now organized resistance of the Bristol, Liverpool and London traders, led by the Royal African Company, had little difficulty in securing this repeal.

---

[25] *Spotswood Letters,* II., 323; *Virginia State Papers,* I., 206. The benefits from this revenue were, according to Spotswood; "finishing a house for the governor, which was little more than begun when the duty was laid, assisting North Carolina with the Indian wars, fortifying our own frontiers, building a public magazine and a prison, contributing towards the building of the church at Williamsburg and paying for the suppression of pyrats." An Emergency Fund of £17,872 still remained from the levies of the colony. Hening, III., 113, 192, 193, 229, 233, 346, 482, 492; Campbell, *Virginia,* 376; *Calendar Virginia State Papers,* I, 123. With the exception of four months then, a continuous duty had been exacted on slaves from April 27, 1699, to June 22, 1708, a period of more than nine years.

[26] *Spotswood Letters,* I., 52, 72; II., 52, 97; Hening, IV., 30.

[27] Jefferson, *Notes on Virginia,* 146.

But the brief enforcement of this act proved a disaster to the colony. The colonists had made the mistake, in their earnest desire to check the trade at once, of not inserting a clause suspending the operation of the act until the royal will was known. This was so offensive in England that the Virginia Governor was instructed not to assent to any future act of the kind unless the suspensory clause were added, and the act of 1723 was forthwith condemned on this excuse and because it was supposed to contract British trade by levying the tax upon the importer. The real reasons for repeal were the royal interests in the slave trade and the alleged fact that the duties were intended to be prohibitive, and actually did restrict importations.[28] The contention as to whether the duty was paid by the importer or by the buyer, which arose between the traders and the Virginia agents, was complicated by an opinion rendered to the Crown that the duty was really paid by the buyer in the increased price paid for his labor, and that the increased cost of production was added to the price of the products sold in England, and thus the tax was ultimately transferred to the English consumer.[29] This tax on trade and lessening of the royal revenues the Crown had no disposition to allow even in the interests of its colonists. For nine years all attempts of the Virginia Assembly to renew the duty on negroes were futile; though, according to Jefferson and Colonel Peter Fontaine, the attempts were constant. Royal assent could not be obtained even to acts containing the flattering suspensory clause.[30]

---

[28] Hening, IV., 119; *Virginia State Papers*, I., 206, 207. Both the "separate" traders and the Company urged that this duty, though only 40 s. a head, was prohibitive, as 15 per cent. of the negroes imported were not worth £5 each, while on the coast of Africa they cost the importer £16, so that the duty was practically from 33 to 50 per cent. *Virginia MSS.*, B. R. O., II., 1723, September 23 to January 17. The Virginia agent showed that the duty was paid by the buyer.

[29] *Virginia MSS.*, B. R. O., 1729, October 14.

[30] Hening, IV., February, 1727; Jefferson, *Notes*, 146; Fontaine, *Huguenot Family*, 352. Thus the act of 1727 was revoked by the king, and in 1729

2

In 1732 circumstances arose that enabled the colony to obtain a 5 per cent. *ad valorem* duty on negroes, to be paid by the buyer. Both of these points, the duty on the gross sale and payment by the purchaser, were concessions to the contentions of the Royal African Company, and the Assembly further abased itself by "most humbly beseeching" the Crown that the law be enacted [31] for the absolutely necessary revenues of the government, as the people would not submit to a direct tax by the poll. Other considerations fortunately were present to influence a favorable decision. The Royal African Company in 1730 had succeeded in extorting a bonus from Parliament which was far more valuable than its trade in Virginia, and the Crown's immediate interest in the duties was lessened. To protect the exclusive Company Parliament had laid a tax on the importations of other traders, when the trade was opened to competition in 1698. The duties in Virginia had seemed not only to lower the profits of the African Company but to limit the receipts of the tax due from these traders, and two additional reasons had thus been afforded for repeal of the Virginia laws. In 1730, however, the African Company, which had not proven a successful competitor with the other traders, obtained a grant of £10,000 [32] a year for their previous loss for nearly twenty years, in lieu of the duty paid by the traders, which was now abolished. This made the Company independent of the Virginia trade, and it no longer had reason to oppose duties on a business from which it was practically excluded. Another

---

the Board of Trade instructed the colony to substitute other duties for those on negroes. In 1730 the colonists begged to be allowed to lay a duty on liquors, as the people would not submit to a poll-tax. This was refused then, but was finally conceded in 1732.

[31] In no other bills except these for duties on liquor and slaves do such clauses of appeal occur as; "We most humbly beseech your Majesty" in your "great wisdom," etc., etc.

[32] Brock, *Virginia Historical Society Collections*, VII., prefatory note to fourth exclusive charter of the Royal African Company.

reason which tended to change the policy of the Crown, was its anxiety to conciliate the colonists as much as possible in order to enforce its scheme of commercial monopoly and to crush out incipient colonial manufactures, which at this time were giving fresh alarm.[33] It was essential to this scheme that the agricultural colonies, at least, chief amongst which was Virginia, be exclusively confined to the economic line marked out by the interests of the home country.

In the light of these facts we can understand the permission to revive duties on slaves in 1732 and their continuance by successive acts practically unbroken until the Revolution. From 1732 to 1778, when the importation of slaves was prohibited by the State of Virginia, duties, constantly increasing in amount, were effective, except for a brief period of about six months after August 1, 1751, when the act of 1732, which had been continued by amendments, was inadvertently allowed to expire.[34] The Assembly generally took especial care to avoid such lapse. The acts had usually a duration limited to four years, and two years and sometimes longer before they expired they were continued by other acts in order that no possible hitch might come from delay of the royal assent and lapse of the duty. Every effort possible was made to discourage slave importations. A drawback of the full amount of the duty was now allowed when the slave was exported out of the colony within twelve months, and this exportation was not to be to North Carolina, as it was too easy for the slaves to be smuggled back from there. The strictest regulations were made for the prompt collection of the duty, and the fact that it was laid on the buyer, would in itself, it was hoped, discourage purchases. Every attempted evasion by factors, traders and shipmasters was met as it arose and carefully provided against for the future; even the

[33] Rabbeno, *American Commercial Policy*, 20.
[34] Hening, IV., 317, 320, 394, 474; V., 28. See acts of 1733, 1734, 1738, 1740, 1742, 1745, 1747 and special acts of 1736, 1740.

privileged slaves of shipmasters though unsold were held liable to the duty.[35]

Whenever an occasion arose in which England was compelled to ask aid of her colony, such as troubles with the Spanish, French, or Indians, it was immediately seized upon as a pretext by the Assembly to increase duties or to levy extra tariffs. Thus when the coöperation of colonial troops was demanded in 1740 for the expedition against Carthagena an addition of 5 per cent. *ad valorem* over the existing 5 per cent. duty was exacted for the colonial expenses. This duty was significantly laid upon slaves and not upon liquors. The pressure was administered, however, by the Assembly in the form of a "most humble" petition to the Crown. Again, in 1752, when it was desired to renew the lapsed duties, the pretext offered was the public debts of the French war; and next the defense of the western frontier against the encroachments of the French was used for the further addition of a 5 per cent. duty in 1754 and of a 10 per cent. duty in 1755, each for three years.[36] This latter duty was continued in 1757 for seven years longer as an "aid to His Majesty" in defense of the colony. So for fully five years, May, 1755, to May, 1760, the tax of a 20 per cent. *ad valorem* duty, and for three years 25 per cent., was enforced upon slaves. This slave impost, together with a discriminating tax of 4 *s.* 6 *d.* on negro tithables, 2 *s.* more than on white, was practically prohibitive of the slave trade, and, consequently, on the ground that importation was checked and revenue defeated, the Crown again demanded the repeal of the two exceptional 10 per cent. duties.[37]

England was now in a position to dispense with colonial

---

[35] One reason why the payment by buyers had been opposed in Virginia was on account of the trouble of collection, which was overcome with difficulty. Hening, IV., 474; V., 28, 30.

[36] Hening, V., 92, 112; VI., 219, 220, 355; *Dinwiddie Papers*, II., 86.

[37] *Ibid.*, VI., 355, 419, 466, 467; VII., 363, 383, 640. The repeals were made in 1760 and 1761.

aid and to give attention to her trade interests. The French war was practically ended. Fort Duquesne had fallen in 1758 and Quebec in 1759. The Virginians appreciated the situation, submitted to the repeal, and contented themselves with continuing a 5 per cent. duty by successive acts until the workings of Grenville's policy had produced such a general state of resistance in the colonies that Virginia could boldly again apply pressure and revive exceptional duties.[38]

Though the colony could not protect itself from English traders, it was allowed to do so from American traders, who operated from the West Indies or from Maryland and North Carolina, as the restriction of these was wholly beneficial to the English trade. A heavy duty of 20 per cent. *ad valorem* was consequently permitted on these importations from 1759 to 1773.[39] In 1766 the Assembly again became bold enough to lay a duty of 10 per cent. for seven years in addition to that of 5 per cent. which was continued for three years, for the avowed purpose of lessening the poll tax merely. In 1769 this additional duty was continued until 1776, because, said the Assembly, "it was found expedient," and a further 5 per cent. duty was also revived. In 1772 these duties were all continued until the 20th of April, 1778, so that the effective duty on slaves from the African coast, Maryland, and North Carolina was 20 per cent., while on West India slaves it was as much as 40 per cent of their value.[40]

---

[38] A letter from Colonel Peter Fontaine to his brother, in 1757, well illustrates the attitude of the English to the imposition of duties, "which," he says, "they wink at while we are in danger of being torn from them, but we dare not do it in time of peace." "Our Assembly," he continues, "foreseeing the evil consequences of importing such numbers [of slaves] hath often attempted to lay a duty upon them which would amount to a prohibition, such as £10 or £20 a head, but no governor dare pass such a law, having instructions to the contrary from the Board of Trade at home. This plainly shows the African hath the advantage of the colonies."

[39] Hening, VII., 338, 340; VIII., 192, 337. This duty was imposed by acts of 1759, 1766, and 1769.

[40] Hening, VIII., 191, 237, 337, 531, 532; cf. Tucker, *Blackstone*, I., 51.

In the language of these enactments we find a growing spirit of independence on the part of the Assembly and a disposition to admit candidly, now that fear of coercion was lessened, its intent to prohibit the slave trade. The duties did not however, effectively prohibit, and in 1772, after two months trial of the combined acts, the House of Burgesses was forced to address a direct petition to the Throne. The language of this petition is so significantly prophetic that it should be briefly quoted. " We implore," it says, " your Majesty's paternal assistance in averting a calamity of a most alarming nature. The importation of slaves into the colonies from the coast of Africa hath long been considered as a trade of great inhumanity, and under its present encouragement we have too much reason to fear will endanger the very existence of your Majesty's American dominions. We are sensible that some of your Majesty's subjects may reap emoluments from this sort of traffic, but when we consider that it greatly retards the settlement of the colonies with more useful inhabitants and may in time have the most destructive influence, we presume to hope that the interest of a few will be disregarded when placed in competition with the security and happiness of such numbers of your Majesty's dutiful and loyal subjects. We therefore beseech your Majesty to remove all those restraints on your Majesty's governors in this colony which inhibit their assenting to such laws as might check so pernicious a consequence." To this appeal no attention was paid in England.[41] The Secretary of State curtly said that no answer would be given.

So general in Virginia was the odium of the policy that forced negro slavery and population upon the colonies, that Jefferson, voicing the sentiments of his people, inserted a severe arraignment of England's king in the first draft of the Declaration of Independence for inciting the negroes to arms,

---

[41] *Journal of the House of Burgesses,* 131; Tucker, *Blackstone,* pt. II., v. 1, app., 52.

" those very negroes," he said, " whom by an inhuman use of his negative he hath refused us permission to exclude by law." [42]    The same clause previously inserted in the preamble of the first constitution of the State in 1776, and continued in every Virginia constitution to the present day, is a living witness of the Virginians' sincere contempt for what they termed one of the chief acts of the " detestable and insupportable tyranny " of the Mother Country, and justified their revolt from her authority.    The forced importation of convicts and slaves was then not an unimportant cause of the change of sentiment in the peculiarly loyal colony of Virginia [43] that won her support of the Revolution.

One of the first acts of Virginia as a sovereign State was the emphatic prohibition of the slave trade, enforced by the exaction of such penalties and oaths from traders or immigrants that few might hope to evade the law. [44]   This act was passed by her first Assembly in 1778, thirty years before Great Britain took like measures, and before the operation of the prohibition of the United States, delayed by the interests of New England and some of the Southern States.   Virginia thus had the honor of being the first political community in the civilized modern world to prohibit the pernicious traffic. Her course of action was probably at first determined by fear of the effects of increased negro population upon domestic and political institutions, rather than by sentimental disapproval of the institution of slavery, a disapproval not general with Englishmen of that early day.   As late as 1793 the migra-)

---

[42] Hening, I., 50.

[43] *Virginia Constitution*, 1878, 66; Ellis, *Debates*, III., 452, 454; Jefferson, *Works* (Ford ed.), II., 11, 52, 53; Franklin, *Works* (Bigelow ed.), IV., 108, 254.  The clause was probably the work of George Mason and Jefferson.

[44] Hening, IX., 471, 472; cf. XIII., 62.   The penalty to the importer was £1,000, and to the trader and seller £500 and the freedom of the slave. A solemn oath was required of every settler that he imported no slaves for sale and had owned none bought since the passage of the Act.

tion or importation of free negroes and mulattoes into the State was prohibited under the heavy penalty of £100. Yet in the late years of the eighteenth century the opposition to the institution of slavery itself had so far advanced in Virginia as to suggest that it may have rendered effective support even earlier to the demand for the exclusion of slaves. In 1788 the reduction of the children of free blacks and mulattoes to slavery was made a crime punishable by death without benefit of clergy, and this was soon followed by the propositions of George Tucker and Jefferson for a general emancipation of slaves.[45]  Political and social conditions that might result from the presence of and contact with an enormous body of freed men was an insurmountable barrier to the realization of such wishes.  The incubus imposed by English and American greed through a long series of years could not be removed at a single stroke, however earnest the desire of the wisest and most far-sighted Virginians.

To appreciate this fact it is only necessary to revert to the continued growth of African population, which all the efforts of the colonists had been unable to check.  From the middle of the century, when the African population was 120,156 to 173,316 whites, it had steadily increased until 1782, when there were 270,762 slaves to 296,852 free persons, and the blacks were consequently possibly equal to or more numerous than the whites.  Importations had not even then ceased, and Jefferson declared ; " This blot on our country increases as fast or faster than the whites." [46]

After 1723 the negro population had constantly gained upon the white, but it had now, or certainly within the next few years, reached its highest proportion to the total population, *i. e.*, over 50 per cent.  With the prohibition of the slave trade, although the domestic increase was great, its ratio

---

[45] Hening, XII., 531; Statutes at Large, 1793, n. s., I., 239; Tucker, *Slavery in Virginia.*
[46] Jefferson, *Notes*, 329, 334.

began to decline, and in 1790 it had fallen to 40.9 per cent. In the next decade it rose again to 41.6 per cent. and continued to rise until between 1820 and 1830, when the slave population was 39.9 per cent., and the ratio of negroes was 43.4 per cent. But from that point the ratio declined steadily to the outbreak of the war between the States, when it was scarcely 37 per cent. The cause of the rise in the early nineteenth century was not importation, which had practically ceased, but the enormous domestic natural increase, which raised the slave population from 293,427 in 1790 to 469,757 in 1830. Between 1830 and 1840 there was an actual decline to 448,987 slaves, owing to the opening of the great Southwest to cotton. This gave rise to a large domestic slave trade from Virginia and the old slave States which tended to carry off the natural increase. It was estimated in 1831 that Virginia sent annually as many as 6,000 slaves to the other Southern States.[47] After the panic of 1841, which restricted this outlet, the slave population again began to rise, and in 1850 there were 472,528 slaves in Virginia, though the whites were now increasing vastly out of proportion to the blacks. In 1860 there were 490,865 slaves and 53,042 free colored persons as compared with 1,047,411 whites.

Virginia, however, remained until the war the most populous of the Southern States in both whites and blacks, though Georgia, Mississippi and Alabama by 1860 were closely approximating her in negro population. Although the negroes in Virginia in 1790 were almost as many as those in Maryland, North Carolina and South Carolina combined, and nearly one-third of the entire black population of the United States, their proportion diminished before the increasing numbers in these States, Georgia, and the new States of

---

[47] Tucker, *Progress of United States*, 17, 22, 27, 35, 45, 55 ; Chase and Sanborn, *North and South*, 20. The highest ratio of the nineteenth century of slaves and blacks to total population was reached in 1820—39.9 per cent. for slaves, and 43.4 per cent. for blacks.

the Southwest.   From 1820 to 1850 the rate of increase of slave population in Virginia was from three to ten times less than in any other Southern State except Maryland, while the continued drain of the domestic slave trade to the South and the emigration of free negroes to the North was reducing her black population to limits comparable with that of many of her sister States.   Though the sentiment for emancipation gained ground constantly from 1790 to 1830, as is shown by the large increase of free negroes, and though the density of population was beginning to produce conditions that economically demanded the extinction of slavery, there was no hope that either emigration or deportation would ever rid the State of the incubus of its African population.   The solution of this problem so earnestly sought and debated by leading men in the eighteenth and early nineteenth centuries, just as that of its prevention had been by their fathers, and like it without result, has passed to the present generation, which, faced by the same insurmountable barriers, has at last accepted the fact of an ever-present negro population and has striven to meet resultant conditions in politics and society to the best of its ability with wisdom and justice.

# CHAPTER II.

## DEVELOPMENT OF SLAVERY.

*Legal Status of the Slave.*—The creation of legal status is dependent locally upon either customary or statutory law, and in the case of organized society usually upon both. It is the result of development rather than of a single specific act, though such an act culminating from a previous development may serve to distinguish sharply the legal condition of one individual from that of another and so mark the progression from one status to another. Status embraces one or more incidents essential to its strict definition, which rest for authority ultimately on custom recognized as law through either judicial decisions or statutory enactments. These incidents may be combined with others, non-essential, which, derived from the same source, vary in number, kind and degree according to the nature of the status fixed, and which are constantly increased and modified as this status approaches its full legal perfection. The addition or modification of some essential incident, however, may at any time involve such important consequences and differences in legal relations as to justify the creation in terms of law of a new status marking the rise of a new institution which, historically, is but a part of a previous institutional growth. This, as will be pointed out, finds illustration in the closely related institutions of servitude and slavery, each with its clearly marked status in law and custom.

In the case of societies politically dependent, as colonies generally are, the status of individuals not pre-determined by the common, or customary law or statute law of the governing community, or by private international law, may be fixed as to its characteristic element, by single acts of the judiciary or legislature, of the sovereign, or even of the dependent body, where such initiative is delegated to it. In these acts either the force of previous custom in the community is recognized or legality is given to the legislation of some other political entity through the adoption of a status determined by it. Both of these methods receive illustration in the imposition of a status by the English and Dutch upon the negroes imported into their American colonies.

The distinguishing mark of the state of slavery is not the loss of liberty, political and civil, but the perpetuity and almost absolute character of that loss, whether voluntary or involuntary in origin. It differs, then, from other forms of servitude limited in place or time, such as mediaeval vassalage, villainage, modern serfdom and technical servitude in degree rather than in kind; its other incidents being very similar and in many cases even identical with theirs. In the civil right of personal freedom the slave alone has no part, but in other social rights, such as personal security and the right to private property, the slave might, and in almost all historic cases did, participate to a limited extent together with the vassal, villain, serf and servant.

The first negroes introduced into the North American Colonies, that is, those early brought to the Bermudas and to Virginia, do not seem to have been slaves in the strict sense of the term. As the captives, not of warfare, but of piracy, they were under the protection of international law in maintaining their original status, and had they been citizens of a powerful civilized community they might have received it. They were, no doubt, slaves or captives of the Spanish, but no rights of ownership, even if just, could pass to the nation by whom they were made a prize of piracy. The masters of the Dutch and English privateers, therefore, had no rights of ownership which they could legally exercise or transfer over the negroes imported until rights were recognized by the law of England or of the Bermudas and Virginia. Until this recognition came, the negroes were persons of undetermined status to whom the privileges of the common law were not specifically extended. If the term slavery can be used at all to describe their condition it is only in the sense of political as distinguished from domestic slavery; that is, dependence upon the state similar to the plebeian at Rome and the helot at Sparta, a condition from which the majority of the Virginians had as a matter of fact, though not of law, just emerged in 1619, and in which the people of the Bermudas still to a certain extent remained. Domestic slavery could[1] find no sanction until the absolute ownership in the bodies of the negroes was vested by lawful authority in some individual. The first step in this direction was not made until 1623 in the Bermuda Islands, and it was not until 1625 that a case involving similar action arose in Virginia.[2]

---

[1] Compare Tucker's view in his " *Slavery in Virginia*," 17–22.

[2] Prior to this the negroes were legally but colony servants, and a disposition to recognize them as such seems apparent. Both in the Bermudas and in Virginia public provisions were exchanged for them in the first instance, and they were put to work upon public lands to support the governor and other officers of the government; or, as were several in Virginia, they were put into the hands of representative planters closely connected with the government in order to separate them from one another. The plan was that probably reproduced in Providence Island, where in 1633 (*Calendar State Papers*, p. 160, 162, 167, 229) it was recommended that twenty or thirty negroes be introduced for public works, and that they should be separated among various families of officers and industrious planters to prevent the formation of plots. Some of these negroes received wages and purchased their freedom, and the length of servitude seems to have been dependent on the time of conversion to Christianity (*Ibid.*, 202).

In 1623, according to the census taken and preserved in " *Lists of Living and the Dead in Virginia*" (February 16, 1623) (*Colonial Records of Virginia*, 37, *et seq.*), it appears that the twenty-three negroes living prior to April preceding were distributed among seven distinct settlements: at Fleur de Hundred, eleven; at Warrasqueak, four; at James' City, three; at Elizabeth City, two, and at three outlying plantations one each. From the muster taken in the next year (1624–25) (Hotten, *Lists*, etc., 218, *et seq.*) the twenty-three negroes then living were distributed in five localities in the possession of seven planters, planters in two cases having property in

In both instances the question settled was that of owner-ship of the right to the services of negroes, not of their per-sons.  In the Bermudas it was vested in individuals, and has the appearance of a full recognition of private ownership in this right.  In Virginia the right was vested in an individual, but under peculiar circumstances, and as the individual was the governor of the colony, it probably involved nothing more than the legal recognition of public ownership[3] which

---

the same place (James City and Elizabeth City).  From a careful com-parison of these lists with documents showing the location of these planters and their plantations in 1623 and 1625, respectively, it seems certain that the persons in possession of the negroes were the same in both years, and doubtless had had control of them from their first introduction in 1619, 1621 and 1623.  There is nothing to suggest that a single transfer of pos-session had taken place after being fixed, though in several cases the negroes had been moved from one place or plantation to another by their possessors.  Not more than three instances of this even seem to have occurred : (1) three women were removed probably from Governor Yeard-ley's property at Fleur de Hundred to his place at Jamestown ; (2) a child and its mother (Peter and Frances) were transferred from Warrasqueak to Abraham Piercey's estate, called Piercey Hundred ; (3) John, a body-servant, probably of Captain West's, accompanied him on his removal from a plantation opposite to James City to Elizabeth City, where he was settled on the company's land.  (Brown, *Genesis*, II., 1087.)  It is a significant fact that the seven possessors of the negroes were all officers of the govern-ment except two in 1625 ; *i. e*, Bennet, a London merchant owning a large plantation in Virginia, and Captain William Pierce, a member of the Council for Virginia in 1631, and all except three in 1619.  (R. Kingsmill), councilor, in 1625–6, Bennet and Pierce.)  Of the possessors of 1619 one was Governor Yeardley ; one a burgess, Tucker ; one cape merchant, Piercey ; and one, Captain West, a Councilman.  (Brown, *idem*, II., 1047 ; Lefroy, *Bermudas*, I., 252, 281.)

[3] Lefroy, *Bermudas*, I., 281 ; Jefferson, *Reports*, Case of Brass ; Neil, *Virginia Carolorum*, 33.  In the Bermudas negroes were at this time divided amongst masters by the governing authorities.  Whether this involved full ownership of their services or was only in the nature of a lease of public servants by the colony is not quite clear.  In Virginia the celebrated case of the negro Brass is cited erroneously by Jefferson as the first instance of fixing the status of the negro slave.  Brass was brought in on a ship, and seems to have been the personal servant of the master of the

custom and official action had previously sanctioned in the case of former negroes. In each case the legal right conferred was that of *possessio* and not of *dominium*, and in the absence of specification to the contrary it was of limited duration and consequently lacked the most essential elements of a state of slavery. The subsequent action of the possessors shows that the legal limitations were recognized and observed.

Whatever may have been the intent and hope of the persons in possession of the negroes as regards their ultimate enslavement, no attempt to do so legally seems for a long time to have been made. Though the practice and incidents of negro and Indian slavery in the Spanish colonies were perfectly familiar to the people of Virgina, for some reason the notion of enslavement gained ground but slowly, and although the conditions surrounding a negro or Indian in possession could easily make him a *de facto* slave, the colonist seems to have preferred to retain him only as a servant. This was largely the result of the developing institution of servitude which in the early years of the seventeenth century adequately met the economic demands of colonial society, and for social and moral reasons was preferable to any system of slavery, and particularly to that of negroes and Indians.

The primary steps in the institutional development which culminated in slavery are then to be found in the legislation, customary and statutory, that defined that condition of persons legally known as servitude.[4] Servitude not only preceded slavery in the logical development of the principle of subjection, standing mid-way between freedom and absolute subjection, but it was the historic base upon which slavery, by

---

vessel. The master having died, the question of the ownership of Brass was raised. The general court of Virginia decided that rather than vest him as a slave in the hands of the ship's company, it would assign him to the governor of the colony.

[4] For a full discussion of the origin and development of this institution see the author's *White Servitude in Virginia*, Johns Hopkins University Studies in Historical and Political Science, thirteenth series.

the extension and addition of incidents, was constructed.
Developed itself from a species of free contract-labor, by the
peculiar conditions surrounding the importation of settlers
and laborers into the English-American colonies, servitude
was first applied to whites and then to negroes and Indians.
It began to receive legal definition as soon as colonial law
became operative in 1619, at the very time that the first
importations of negroes were made. It was but natural then
that they should be absorbed in a growing system which
spread to all the colonies and for nearly a century furnished
the chief supply of colonial labor. Negro and Indian servitude thus preceded negro and Indian slavery, and together
with white servitude in instances continued even after the
institution of slavery was fully developed.

Virginia was not the only colony in which servitude bore
this direct relation to slavery as its preparatory stage or form.
Negro and Indian servitude passed historically into slavery
in most of the English-American colonies, if not in all. This
is certainly true of Maryland, Massachusetts, Rhode Island,
Pennsylvania, Georgia, North Carolina and South Carolina.
In all of these colonies statutory recognition of slavery, though
tending to be anticipated by customary or judicial sanction,
was postponed for sometime after the introduction of the subjects of slavery, who were consequently referred to a different
status.[5]

Most of the incidents developed in servitude were passed
on to slavery, some of them modified and amplified to con-
form to the changed relations, but the numerous acts on the
statute books applying equally to servants and slaves show
that the similarity and very essential connection of the two
institutions continued while they existed side by side. The
period of the chief legal development of servitude was natur-

---

[5] Hurd, *Law of Freedom and Bondage*, I., 248, 249, 257, 260, 262, 268, 269,
note 275, 289, 295, 297, 310. Laws relating to servants and slaves; *Robinson MSS.*, 10, 12; Accomac Records, 2.

ally prior to the recognition of slavery, but even after the transition to slavery had been effected, and through the whole time that the two institutions were coexistent, that is, for more than a century in Virginia, Massachusetts, Maryland and Connecticut, and for long periods in the other colonies, the reciprocal influence of the one on the other was marked. The general effect of this relation is to be seen in the gradual hardening of the conditions of servitude and mitigation of those of slavery, so that the form finally assumed by slavery was of a milder type than ancient, mediæval, or even contemporary forms of that institution, while the line between servitude and slavery tended constantly toward obliteration.[6]

Servitude, occupying a primary position in colonial development, was as regards its principles largely the product of customary law. It was a condition unknown to the common law of England, and had to depend in the first instance for its sanction and definition on the growing body of colonial common law, supplemented by colonial statutes where unity and exactness were demanded by the growing complexity of incidents as institutional development proceeded. Owing to the simplicity of the relations of master and servant and the ability of colonial courts to regulate the rules applying to it, few statutes were called for before the middle of the seventeenth century, but from that point forward the urgent necessity for legal uniformity, now threatened by the varying practices of the judiciary, could only be met by legislative action.[7] It was in this period of growing statutory regulation that occasion arose for strictly defining the status of slavery. Slavery consequently in Virginia, Massachusetts, and a number of the colonies rested for its earliest general sanction upon statute, and was in its future development very largely the

---

[6] Compare here the lengthening of the terms of servitude and the frauds by which the attempt was made to turn the servant into a *de facto* slave. *White Servitude in Virginia*, 68.

[7] *Ibid.*, 42.

3

product of statutory law.  As an institution it was, like servitude, purely a colonial development not determined nor affected
by the law of England, although slavery, unlike servitude, was
recognized by the Mother Country and in general found a
sanction in international as well as in municipal law.  In this,
however, Virginia and the other colonies differed from New
York, where the doctrines of the civil law as enforced in
Holland, and not colonial law, were first applied to sanction
slavery.[8]

The language of legislative recognition in the several
colonies indicates the essential element in the change of status.
The first general sanction of slavery in Virginia was by an
Act of Assembly, March, 1661, stating that "negroes are
incapable of making satisfaction [for the time lost in running
away] by addition of time."[9]  Addition to the time of service was the customary punishment inflicted upon servants
for this offense.  So the Maryland law, c. 30, 1663, declared
that "all negroes or other slaves shall serve *durante vita.*"
The Massachusetts Fundamentals of 1641 proscribed " bond
slavery, villenage," and "captivity," except of "captives
taken in war," and of such strangers "as willingly sell themselves or are sold."  "And those shall have all the liberties
and Christian usages which the laws of God established in
Israel concerning such persons doth morally require," said
the law.  Virginia, then, so far from being the first American colony to sanction domestic slavery, as has been generally
believed, was in reality but the third, being preceded by both
Massachusetts and Connecticut.  Statutory recognition of
slavery by the American colonies occurred as follows : Massachusetts, 1641; Connecticut, 1650; Virginia, 1661; Maryland, 1663; New York and New Jersey, 1664; South Carolina, 1682; Pennsylvania and Rhode Island, 1700; North

---

[8] There were, it is said, 15,000 slaves (negroes) in England in 1772.
Hurd, *Law of Freedom and Bondage,* I., 178–192, 260, 356–371.
[9] Hening, II., 26 ; cf. *Ibid.,* I., 538- 540.

Carolina, 1715, and Georgia, 1755.[10]   Prior to these dates the
legal status of all subject negroes was that of servants, and
their rights, duties, and disabilities were regulated by legislation the same as, or similar to, that applied to white servants.

This was true also of the subject Indian up to 1670 in
Virginia, when an act reduced the few Indians that might be
imported by sea, presumably from the West Indies or the
Spanish main, to a state of slavery.[11]   The great body of
Indian subjects being native, however, remained servants up
to 1676, when in the exigencies of the Indian war captives
were made slaves by one of Bacon's laws.   Before this time
no native Indian, whether a child sold by its parents or a
captive of warring tribes could be legally held as a slave.
Acts were passed in 1655 and in 1661 specifically prohibiting
Indian slavery and guaranteeing to such Indians all the rights
of English servants.   When the attempt was made to reduce
them to slavery freedom might readily be obtained by appeal
to the courts.[12]   In 1682 Indian slavery was extended to captives sold by tributary Indians in the hope of mitigating their
condition, as it was certain that they would be held in slavery
by their captors.   In 1691, however, Indian slavery was
finally abolished by Law.[13]

The legal first enslavement of Indians covered a much
shorter period in our history than that of negroes.   In two

---

[10] Hurd, *Law of Freedom and Bondage*, I., 249, 257, 260, 262, 265, 266, 268,
269, 275, 276, 283, 288, 289, 295–297, 310.   The use of the term "negro
slaves" by the act of 1659–60 encouraging Dutch importations was no
sanction of the institution, but merely referred to the usage of the term by
the Dutch.

In the Bermudas slavery seems to have existed as early as 1629 and
certainly by 1648.   Lefroy, *Bermudas*, I., 463, 483, 500, 505, 633.

[11] Hening, II., 280, 283.

[12] Hening, II., 346, 404; *White Servitude*, 40, note.   This was one of
Bacon's acts, but it was subsequently affirmed by the Assembly; Henrico
Records, 41, 57.

[13] Hening, I., 396, 471; II., 69, 163, 155.

colonies, Virginia and Pennsylvania, it was confined to less than a quarter of a century, and in Virginia alone it was limited wholly to the seventeenth century. In at least two others, Rhode Island and North Carolina, it existed for less than half a century, and in the remaining colonies it extended but little over this. By 1715 the importation of Indian slaves into New England was generally prohibited, or was discouraged by duties, as in New Jersey. This result has a natural explanation in the fact that the Indian proved an unprofitable and dangerous subject of slavery. He was of little economic benefit, was unruly and immoral, inciting the other Indians, and was a serious discouragement to the importation of white labor in the form of servants. After the Tuscaroras war in the South the source of slavery by capture was largely cut off, and Indian slavery, except as supported by heredity, generally declined.

The recognition of Indian and negro slavery in customary law came somewhat earlier than that of statute. In Massachusetts and Connecticut Pequod captives were spared, and treated, as captives generally were under the sanction of *jus gentium*, as perpetual servants. They were sold to other Indians or to the island and mainland colonies of England as early as 1637, thus marking the first small beginnings of a domestic slave trade. Negroes as articles of exchange or purchase were introduced early in 1638, and some of these seem to have been by custom reduced to slavery as well as to its consequence, slave-breeding. So, too, in Rhode Island, the practice of buying negroes " for service or slaves forever " was common in 1652. No legal authority for this status, however, yet existed in positive legislative acts. The earliest sanction in local law was a ruling of the Massachusetts General Court in 1639 confirming a title to slaves specifically. The status servitude, on the contrary, had distinct recognition even in statute law by 1630–36 in Massachusetts, by 1643 in Connecticut, and by 1647 in Rhode Island. This was also the case in Virginia by 1619, in Maryland by 1637, in North

Carolina by 1665, in Pennsylvania by 1682, and in Georgia by 1732, so that ample time was allowed in many cases for the local definition of this institution before slavery entered upon either its customary or legal development.[14]

In the circumstances surrounding the enactments defining slavery the natural transition of servitude into slavery is apparent. Particularly is this the case with regard to negroes in Virginia, Maryland and Massachusetts. The first essential element in the change of status consisted merely in the modification of an incident, the extension of the term of service from a period of years to that of natural life. What is termed perpetual was substituted for limited service, while all the predetermined incidents of servitude, except such as referred to ultimate freedom, continued intact. This fact was recognized in the common language of subsequent law, which frequently employed the terms "servant for life," "perpetual servant," and "bond servant" (bound servant) interchangeably with "slave," and joined the names "servant" and "slave" and their liabilities in the same enactments. Apparently there was no marked change of condition either practically or legally as regarded the individual. The master acquired an extension of his right to service and a resulting extension of his obligation of protection and maintenance. The slave lost his right to ultimate liberty but gained the more valuable right of protection for his life and person.[15] It was but the realization in the case of a special class of servants of an aim that had included all in the various attempts to lengthen and constantly renew terms of service so as to provide for continuous subjection, which, if successful, would have resulted in practical life servitude and ultimate slavery. The advantages of

---

[14] Steiner, *Slavery in Connecticut,* 9, 10; Hurd, *Law of Freedom and Bondage,* I., 229, 247, 257, 269, 287; Fowler, *Status of the Negro in Connecticut,* p. 12, says negro slavery existed in New Haven in 1644; *Plymouth Col. Records,* I., 70, 71; Bassett, *Slavery in North Carolina,* 78; Moore, *Slavery in Massachusetts,* 2, 9, 11, 15.

[15] *Winder MSS.,* I., 245.

this from the point of view of the master in the fixity and
certainty of a labor supply and extension of the right of control were so apparent as readily to gain the support of public
sentiment when (the class of servants affected were generally
regarded as a menace to society if free and uncontrolled.)
Consequently, as this unassimilated and dangerous element
was increased by the processes of Indian warfare or of the
African trade, the demand seemed just and necessary for a
legal extension of the master's power to the full limit of control claimed by the possessors of the servant's person before
their transfer to third parties.

But a more important element of the change of status
effected by the several enactments was the extended personal
application given both to the modified and other incidents of
servitude. They were held to attach *ipso facto* to the issue
of perpetual servants where both parents were of this status.
To cover other cases additional provision was made at the
time or implied by the statute, or was subsequently enacted
designating the parent that conferred status upon the offspring.
Such a principle of heredity was wholly foreign at that time to
the condition of servitude, and broadly differentiated it from
the system which resulted. This first doctrine of slavery, as
it might be called, was a natural effect of the conditions of
perpetual service, rather than an inference from a legal conception of the absolute dominion of the master in his slave
and the consequent inability of the slave to hold property
separate from his master; ideas which had not yet developed
in colonial law, however well known they may have been to
the Roman lawyers and to the common-law which supported
English villainage.[16] It was evident that parents under an
obligation of life service could make no valid provision for the
support of their offspring, and that a just title to the service

---

[16] Vinogradoff, *Villainage in England*, 45, 47, 59; Muirhead, *Roman Law*,
40, 120, 126, 127; Justinian, *Institutes*, Lib., I., Tit. 3, sec. 4. "*Servi aut
nascuntur aut fiunt—fiunt ex jure gentium aut jure civili.*"

of the child might rest on the master's maintenance, a principle which was later commonly applied in cases of bastardy in servitude. The origin of this doctrine in the Roman law of slavery is not certain. It is not definitely ascribed there either to *jus civile* or *jus gentium*, but whatever its sanction its existence probably had a like natural explanation. Though direct influence of Roman law principles is not to be inferred, it is an interesting fact that as soon as issue appeared from parents differing in status, the doctrine *partus sequitur ventrem* was evolved, specifically or by implication, in the statutes or customary law of a number of the colonies, while the English common law principles of villainage, deriving status from the father, was specifically enjoined only in Maryland. This involved an important addition to the subjects of slavery in the larger portion, if not the whole, in some cases, of the mulatto class. The order of this important extension of status to further subjects by *statute* was Virginia, 1662; Maryland, 1663; Massachusetts, 1698; Connecticut and New Jersey, 1704; Pennsylvania and New York, 1706; South Carolina, 1712.; Rhode Island, 1728; North Carolina, 1741.[17]

The modification and extension, then, of a single incident of servitude produced a condition of persons that involved momentous consequences. It led almost naturally, and under subsequent environment, necessarily, to that great body of legislation which enters into our historic concept of slavery. It was the point of institutional divergence, if one is to be sought, where slavery began a course of development more or less independent of the system of servitude from which it descended.

The most important legal incidents developed in servitude prior to this time and passed on to slavery were those connected with the growing conception of property in the servant's

---

[17] Hurd, *Law of Freedom and Bondage*, I., 262, 276, 281, 283, 284, 295, 299; Moore, *Slavery in Massachusetts*, 25; Bassett, *Slavery in North Carolina*, 29.

person.   This conception of property right had passed from a
basis of pure personality where it was but a right to service,
resting upon expressed or implied contract between legal persons, to one in which the servant was practically regarded
and treated as personal estate.   As personalty he was, for
instance, rated in inventories of estates, was transferable both
*inter vivos* and by will, descended to the executors and
administrators, and was taxable for tithes.   As a contractural
person he was subject to corporal punishment, to damages for
breach of contract and to a poll tax, while his rights included
a limited personal freedom, the possession of property and
protection within the terms of his contract.   With the loss of
the ultimate right to freedom, the contractural element and
the incidents essential to it were swept away, and as the idea
of personality was obscured, the conception of property gained
force, so that it became an easy matter to add incidents more
strictly defining the property right and insuring its protection.
Consequently the early transition of the slave from personal
estate to a chattel real, or real estate with accompanying incidents, was easy and natural

To this development the status of dependent labor in later
Roman and English law presents an interesting contrast.
The rigid theoretical conception of the slave in *jus gentium*
and *jus civile* as a mere chattel, a thing, without activity of
body or mind except as the agent of his master, and absolutely
under his *dominica potestas*, gave way under the doctrines of
*jus naturale* to a recognition of his personality and his right
to legal protection, and, finally, under Justinian to a large
extension of the milder condition of the colonate which carried
personal freedom to the subject though he was still tied to the
soil, *adscriptus glebae*, like the English villain, but had only
the general disabilities of the later serfs.   So in England free
contract labor tended to supplant Norman villainage at a
comparatively early date.   The social disturbances of the
fourteenth century gave the system of villainage its death
blow, and by the time of English-American colonization,

though an isolated case was pleaded in the courts as late as 1618, the system was practically non-existent, and could not influence American development.

The agrarian reform so produced in England was not wholly successful. It developed free laborers, but they were landless freemen and they were worse off economically than if they had been kept in a semi-servile condition. The capitalist farmer swallowed up the small farmer and increased the number of landless laborers. Under the numerous statutes of laborers down to Elizabeth's Statute of Apprentices in 1565, which summed them all up, these laborers were forced into apprenticeships under hard masters. They had fixed wages, fixed hours of labor, and fixed terms of service. Their labor was free only in the sense of freedom of contract. They might choose at what they would work and under whom, and at what regulated wage and terms; and the master, on his part, was held as strictly accountable for compliance with the terms of the contract as the laborer. This system remained until the industrial revolution which followed the introduction of machinery.

Though under different circumstances such a system might have been transferred bodily to the new colonies, the poverty of the commercial companies undertaking the first settlement, and inability to make good their title to large land possessions prevented the immigration of capitalist farmers with their laborers, and a system conforming to conditions had to be adopted. After passing through several stages of development : the emigrant stockholder who contracted for a term of service for transportation and a share in profits; involuntary service enforced by martial law; penal servitude; and a *metayer* system similar to that of France and Italy, called tenants at halves ;—" indented " or indentured servitude was developed.

Servitude thus, in its colonial origin, was only such a modification of free contract labor in the nature of apprenticeship as was demanded by the peculiar double relation it bore to colonization, being at the same time a labor-supply and an immigration agency.) Similar modifications existed in most of the French colonies and exist to-day with subject labor in British South Africa and in Hawaii. But as the simple relation of master and servant developed, the reciprocal rights and duties of the relation became more complex under the natural demands of environment, and assumed a hardness and fixity comparable only with the incidents of a well-defined social institution such as feudal vassalage. Starting as a free personal relation based on voluntary contract for a definite period of service, in lieu of transportation and maintenance or profit sharing, between poor or venturesome immigrants from Great Britain or the Continent and the individuals or corporations that imported them to America, it tended to pass into a property relation in which (1) was recognized only the involuntary and sometimes indefinite service enjoined by legal authority, judicial or statutory in England or the colonies, or procured by force through an organized system of kidnapping persons in Great Britain, known as "spiriting"; and (2) in which control of varying extent was asserted over the bodies and liberties of the person during service as if he were a thing.[18] The right to the service of both classes, voluntary and involuntary, was supposed to be based upon contract written, verbal, in the form of court decisions, act of assembly or "according to the custom" of the country. This involved a legal fiction in the case of involuntary servants similar to that assumed by Sir Henry Maine to explain the contractural origin of slavery by capture, where a contract is presupposed between the slave and the master, rendering service for the gift of life. The fiction was of importance as it gave the courts, particularly

---

[18] These servants represented all classes, from the highest to the lowest; spendthrifts and younger sons of the nobility and gentry, political prisoners, some Scotch rebels and Irish tories, poor literary and college bred men, "spirited" persons of all degrees, vagrants and convicts for petty crimes, well-to-do German and Swiss peasants who wished to learn farming, and political and religious malcontents.

the local courts, but also the general courts when acting judicially, the right both as to master and servant of defending and enforcing the stipulations of the contract. The decisions of these courts legislated the most important incidents into servitude by crystalizing the customary law on the subject of the relation of master and servant. This judicial action was followed by statutes which strictly defined these incidents and other rights and duties that were to be enforced by the courts. Thus an important step was taken in the institutional development of the relation which ultimately passed in fact, as well as by title, into the relation of master and slave.

With the change of condition, questions demanding legislative settlement rapidly arose and the slave code of Virginia began to assume definiteness. The question of status settled by the act of 1661 applied specifically only to negroes without defining what constituted a negro. There could be no doubt as to the direct issue of negro parents, but when the number of slaves began to increase and immoral relations developed more fully between them and Englishmen in the colony or aboard the transports, serious doubt was expressed as to the status of the offspring. ( In view of the fact that the fear of fornication between a free white woman and a negro was practically absent at that time, the Assembly in 1662 felt safe in enunciating a doctrine of descent similar to the *partus sequitur ventrem* of the Roman law. The offspring was declared to follow the condition of its mother, bond or free, and as far as could be foreseen the entire mulatto population would thus be reduced to slavery or to servitude.[19] To prevent the act from any sign of encouragement to slave breeding by whites, heavy fines, double those in other cases, were laid upon whites committing fornication with negroes.[20]

---

[19] Hening, *Statutes*, 1662, p. 12. This opened the way to an ultimate class of free mulattoes by servant women, though free mulattoes born of free white women must have been very few.

[20] *Ibid.*, II., 170.

Thus by independent local legislation, determined by social exigencies arising from differences of race and color, a second great source of domestic slavery recognized by Roman law, *i. e.*; birth by a slave mother, was affirmed in Virginia, and it became the ultimate means of imposing status upon the majority of the negroes of the South. Of the other two natural sources of slavery, as outlined by Justinian, one, purchase, which had been recognized the year previous, was by far the most common in the seventeenth century and in the eighteenth also, until checked by the decline of the slave trade. From conquest, the third source, the imposition of status was very limited. Captives of warfare in Virginia were comparatively insignificant in number as the principle applied only to Indians between 1676 and 1691.

Notwithstanding its effect it is clear that the purpose of the act of 1662 was primarily punitory. It was designed to prevent race mixture rather than to create slaves. The "spurious issue," as it was termed of whites and blacks was at all times abhorred. In the earliest instances of fornication with negroes, in 1630 and 1640, the severest penalties were inflicted. Whipping and public confession, were exacted of both the offenders in 1640. An additional penalty was imposed upon the female in 1662 of the bondage of her issue, which it was hoped would effectually check the evil. Probably little trouble from the growth of mulattoes was actually experienced until the second half of the century, when both negro and Indian population had greatly increased. The name "mollatoes," of Spanish-American origin, first occurs in an act of 1682, applying only to a class of imported crossbreeds, but by 1691 its extension to a native element seems to have been established. At this time negro and Indian bastards were increasing, and the offense of race mingling had extended even to white women. Thus arose a new difficulty in the clear probability of a class of free mulattoes, but the manner in which the question was disposed of shows conclusively that prevention of an "abominable mixture" and not enslavement was the end in view. Five years servitude was inflicted upon the guilty white woman,[21] and her issue was bound to service for 30 years, apprenticeship being the common and legal mode of dealing with bastardy. Thus by statute was originated a class, probably always small, of mulatto servants, which occupied a position midway between the slave and the ordinary bound servant, and became an ultimate source of the free mulatto. In Virginia the principle of hereditary slavery was never carried to its full logical conclusion. Issue did not uniformly follow the lower status.

The philosophic basis of slavery rests historically either upon race or creed, or both. So far the distinction in the status imposed upon the negroes and Indians and their offspring in America was based upon the natural and ineradicable quality of racial difference. If explanation for slavery is sought beyond the unquestioned exigencies of the actual situation it is to be found in race prejudice, a principle which has constantly worked to reduce to subjection the inferior and weaker race, where two peoples have been brought into close contact. The historic justification of slavery by natural subjection as expressed in the dogma of Athenian philosophy, "one race is born to rule and and another to serve," was sufficient to meet any question of the theoretical or moral basis of slavery that had arisen. But another great principle historically of equal importance in the development of slavery had to be considered; namely, religion. On difference of race and difference of creed ancient and modern slavery alike have rested. The barbarian, the heathen, and the heretic have been through all ages subjects of dominion.

The earliest justification offered by the Portuguese for the recognition of modern African slavery was the salvation of

---

[21] *Robinson MSS.*, 1640, October 17; Hening, II., 146, 170; III., 87. If the offender were a free woman she could pay a fine, £15, in lieu of her service. In case of a white (man or woman) marrying a negro or Indian, bond or free, the white was to be banished forever.

souls. This argument quieted the conscience of Christian Europe and the Christian Church joined hands with the Christian State in the process of enslavement. It is but natural that a theory supported by such reasoning and by common acceptance should appear in the colonies of European States. The English carried its application a step farther than the Spanish Bishop Las Casas, whose notion of humanity at least included the natural rights of Indian natives. It was clear that involuntary slavery of Christians to Christians was inconsistent with the freedom and equality of man involved in the true profession of Christ. From the middle ages the doctrine of the Universal Church worshipping one God, who regarded all men alike, had tended to mitigate the condition of subject classes, and the Reformation had established more fully in doctrines of free grace and democracy a freedom of mind, body, and soul from the trammels of mere formalism and self-constituted authority, and had extended the notion of Christian fellowship and brotherhood. The freedom of Christianity was in theory shared by all members of the Christian State, and the name "Christian," in opposition to "heathen," embraced the inhabitants of a Christian land. Consequently the enslavement of Englishmen or persons born in Christian lands was abhorrent. No such feeling was extended to the heathen, whether Jew, Mohammedan or Indian. Slavery was but a just means to a pious end, the salvation of the soul. But when the heathen slave became a convert, a Christian, the inconsistency of a theory that kept him in subjection was apparent. Baptism thus involved a dilemma. If conferred it sealed the pious end of slavery but freed the Christian slave. On the contrary, if enfranchisement was a possible result, Christianization was certain to be retarded or completely stopped. The wisdom and the conscience of colonial assemblies were equal to the emergency. They held both to their justification and to their slaves. The Virginia Assembly in a law of 1667 presents but a typical example of general colonial action. It settled the question by the naïve declaration, worthy of the metaphysician that rightly separates the spiritual person from bodily form, "Baptisme doth not alter the condition of the person as to his bondage or freedom; in order that diverse masters freed from this doubt may more carefully endeavor the propagation of Christianity."

In 1670, when slaves were for the first time legally designated in Virginia, the benefits of Christianity as to freedom were limited to servants imported from Christian lands.[22] From circumstances which arose later this principle preserved many negroes and mulattoes from slavery. The act was passed to ascertain who were slaves and for what time Indians might be legally held in servitude. It was designed to protect Indians from enslavement. But practically it reduced nearly all negroes imported by sea to slavery, while probably most Indians, as they generally came by land, remained servants, though for exceptionally long terms.

Negroes who had been Christianized before importation, or who were imported from the West Indies or the English colonies, and possibly those who had been reshipped in England were, like Indians, by the terms of the act only servants. They were, however, probably comparatively small in number at that time, as importation, except from Africa direct, was scanty. But they seem to have increased rapidly in the next twelve years, and many a heathen negro, Moor, or mulatto in this period owed his freedom from enslavement to the notion of the territorialization of Christianity, which made even the heathen inhabitant a nominal Christian. Curiously the discrimination involved would have perpetuated a mixed class of Christian and heathen servants had the law continued as specified by the act. But the manifest injustice done to the owners of slaves in other colonies, who lost their

---

[22] Hening, II., 260. The English Courts in 1693 adjudged that trover lay in the case of negroes as they were heathen and rightly detained as slaves (Gelly and Chase, 1., 147).

property if they brought them into Virginia by land, and further, to the negro who was converted after his arrival in Virginia, soon called for the repeal of a principle so clearly inconsistent with the true intent of the law.[23]   Necessity, however, prevented an extension to the other wronged classes of benefits similar to those conferred upon Indians, for it might also have carried the mitigating influence of the act to the large number of negroes discriminated against.

The religious doctrine of freedom inherent in Christianity began to wane as a practical principle and to be supplanted by the more profitable social principle of fundamental racial difference.   So by an act of 1682 the benefits of Christianity as a mode of securing freedom were definitely denied to all negroes, mulattoes, hostile Moors and Turks, and to such Indians as were sold by other Indians as slaves where original heathenism could be affirmed.}   Thus for a second time Indian slavery, and for the first time the slave trade by Indians, were legalized.   For economic and political reasons enslavement could now be more openly justified.   The importation of slaves was beginning to compete with that of servants, and a stricter limitation of the right of freedom, even in the case of servants, showed the growth of this demand.[24]

{Reënacted in the revisal of 1705, the law of 1682 remained the basis of the determination of legal slavery for over half a century, that is to 1748.   Unless then an imported servant

---

[23] Hening, II., 490; 1705, c. 49; 1753, c. 2.   It was a matter of impossibility to extend the benefits of freedom to Christian negroes, as all would become Christians in order to escape enslavement.

[24] Hening, II., 490; 1705, c. 49; 1753, c. 2, 4; Jefferson, *Reports*, 112, note.   The change of sentiment on which this was based, though non-religious, was not wholly irreligious.   It was the common-sense view of the English trader and colonist, based on experience, that religion as applied to the heathen barbarians with whom they had to deal was a veneer little more than skin deep, while color and heredity they thought were in the blood.   If their consciences at all troubled them they were easily quieted by the reflection that they were traders and not missionaries, and that the demand was based on economic necessity.

were a Christian, a term which was interpreted to include the·
children of Christian parents and the natives of a Christian
land, at the. time of his first purchase by a Christian, " freedom in Christ Jesus," regardless of subsequent conversion,
could in no wise be interpreted as favorably affecting his
status.

The nominal test for slavery became original heathenism
and present servitude resting upon the *prima facie* evidence
of importation. The actual discrimination, however, was
racial, as practically no Asiatics or Africans were born of
Christian parentage nor had they come from Christian lands.
Possibly some Indians were saved from enslavement under
the act, as missionary efforts may have brought them by
descent and nativity within the interpretation placed upon the
word Christian. But these must have been very few, as the
title to the service of Indians generally rested either upon the
purchase of Indian captives, all of whom were reduced to
slavery by the act, or upon contract[25] for the service of
children made by the parent to secure their education and
Christianization. This latter class was in itself limited, and
probably few of these children were the offspring of Christian
parents.

As a result of the Indian troubles of Bacon's time the
principle of deportation and enslavement of the captive Indian
had been abandoned since 1676. One of Bacon's laws as
a retaliatory measure had recompensed the misdeeds of the
Indians by reducing the captives to slavery, and when the
revolt was ended a law of the Assembly, first in 1676 and
later in 1679, reaffirmed the principle in an almost literal
transcription, making Indians free booty to the captor. In
this light the change of sentiment that called for Indian

---

[25] Hening, II., 143. The acts of 1654, p. 5; 1655, p. 6; 1657, p. 8; 1661,
p. 2, made provision for binding out children until 25 years of age. They
were specially guarded from being made slaves, and it was illegal to reduce
them to that status.

slavery in 1682 is easily explained. Legal enslavement of Indians was continued for nearly ten years longer, when it was finally prohibited by implication rather than by the terms of the act of 1691, which legalized free trade with all Indians. This act was probably intended, as it was later construed, to acknowledge the free state of all Indian tribes. The General Court was called to pass upon the matter as late as 1777. At that time the evidence of the act of 1691 had been lost sight of, and the Court ruled that no legal enslavement could have taken place later than 1705, as the revisal of that year contained a law for free trade with the Indians which was interpreted as freeing the Indian from future enslavement. Not until twenty-nine years later, 1806, was it discovered that this revised law was only a reënactment of a law of 1691, so it is probable that a number of Indians and their descendants were deprived most unjustly, and by gross negligence, it has been thought, of the rights of freedom actually guaranteed by law.[26] Yet notwithstanding the favorable decision of the

---

[26] Hening, II., 346, 404, 491; III., 69. *Virginia Reports*, 1 Hening & Munford, 137, 138; 2 Hening & Munford, 149. The law of 1691 was sufficiently promulgated at the clerk's offices of the various counties at this time, as is shown by the fact that copies in manuscript existed in Northampton and Accomac counties, and in an edition of Purvis, based on the MSS. in Accomac, it also occurs. It was upon Purvis that Judge Tucker based his opinion in 1806. How the lost record and the ignorance of the General Court in 1777 are to be explained it is impossible to say. If there was official negligence, which seems improbable, it was of a most criminal nature. But even in 1806, the Court was ignorant of the two laws of 1676 and ruled that no Indian could be a slave who was not a descendant of a heathen imported between 1679 and 1691. It is only proper to say, however, that the law of 1691 was susceptible of a different interpretation, and it is barely possible that intent conformed to this, in which case enslavement was just and the ruling of the judiciary was a misconstruction. The legislature may have viewed the act as a treaty with a nation which, *ipso facto*, was recognized as of equal status as to freedom, while the treaty in no wise prevented subsequent enslavement of individuals sold by the nation itself to the whites, or of hostile captives, or of Indians not native North Americans as generally understood.

General Court in 1777, which decided against legal enslavement after 1705, the principle was felt to be so far unsettled that two cases as late as 1792 and 1793 were appealed, though unsuccessfully, from county courts to the Court of Appeals to maintain the right to the service of descendants of Indians enslaved subsequent to the act of 1705. In both cases the appellate court affirmed the judgment of the lower court, which granted freedom, and construed the act of 1705 as repealing all former acts, including even that of 1682.[27]

From the beginning of enslavement popular sentiment as expressed by the legislature and the judiciary had discriminated in favor of the native Indian and against the negro. Never at any time had it demanded the subjection of the Indian race *per se*, as was practically the case with the negro in the first slave act of 1661, but only of a portion of it, and that admittedly a very small portion. This distinction was not based, however, so much upon humanity as upon motives of a practical nature determined by the character and environment of the Indian himself. These, as previously stated, rendered him less fit, both politically and economically, as well as naturally, for continued slavery. In the case of the Indian, then, slavery was viewed as of an occasional nature, a preventive penalty and not as a normal and permanent condition. Consequently, Indian slavery in any important sense was a thing of the past, as far as legislation was concerned, before the most onerous incidents of the status were fully developed, and slavery rapidly assumed a solidarity in regard to the one alien race, the negro, that simplified both the domestic and the legal problems involved.[28]

The third[29] step in the substitution of race for the religious

---

[27] Washington, *Reports*, I., 167, 307 (Coleman *vs.* Dick, *et al.*).

[28] 1 Hening & Munford, 183, Hedings *vs.* Wright.

[29] The first step was denying the efficacy of baptism as a source of freedom; the second was limiting the benefits of Christianity to those imported as Christians in 1670, which, in 1682, was further restricted to those born of Christian parents in a Christian land and first purchased by a Christian.

principle in designating the slave is to be found in the act of 1705, which purported to be but the codification of previous legislation still in force regarding slaves. The act of 1682 was more than reënacted in this act, however; it was modified by language that may have made a material difference in the interpretation as to who were slaves. Negroes and mulattoes were not named in the act, but they were practically the only persons worth accounting that were enslaved by it and, probably, nearly every subsequently imported servant of this race was enslaved, as freedom was now made to depend upon personal Christianity in his native country, or the proof of actual freedom in England, or some Christian country before he was shipped. Turks and Moors in amity with England were excepted, as in the act of 1682. This act cut off from freedom the few negroes and mulattoes who might have been born of Christian parents in England, the Spanish colonies, the English colonies, and other Christian lands, and who had been left free by the act of 1682. Christianity as a test had now been reduced to its lowest terms. Faith in Jesus Christ was a "saving grace" only so far as it was actual and personal in the land of nativity. It was easier for a camel to pass through the eye of a needle than for a negro or mulatto servant thereafter imported into Virginia to escape being made a slave if the law was enforced to its full extent. Such remained the law designating slaves for the next twenty-three years.

Possibly by an inadvertence of the copyist, possibly by intent, this law appeared in the revisal of 1748 with the substitution of the clause "all persons who have been or shall be imported" instead of the phrase "all servants imported." Commenting upon the effect of this change, Jefferson says; "An alteration of a few words indeed, but of the most extensive barbarity. It has subjected to slavery the free inhabitants of the two continents of Asia and Africa (except the small parts of them inhabited by the Turks and Moors in amity with England) and also the aborigines of North and South America—unless the word 'shipped' may avail them.

It even makes slaves of the Jews who shall come from these countries, on whose religion ours is engrafted, and so far as it goes supposed to be founded on perfect verity. Nay, it extends not only to such of those persons as should come here after the act, but also to those who came before and might then be living here in a state of freedom."[30] This provision, notwithstanding its possible interpretation and the unjust *ex post facto* clause, was nevertheless retained in subsequent enactments until after the Revolution. It appears in the act of 1753 and was not repealed until the abolition of the slave trade in 1778.[31]

That it was actually applied to subject any others to slavery than negroes and their offspring cannot be affirmed in the absence of reported cases. The intent, if we may judge from later evidence, seems to have been to draw the line of demarkation definitely on the negro race. The substitution of the word " persons " for " servants " would thus reduce practically all of the race imported, or acting in any capacity short of actual freedom in a Christian land, to a state of slavery. This appears probable from the subsequent treatment of the dilemma which was raised by the logical inconsistency with the idea of slavery of the Virginia Declaration of Rights, unanimously adopted in 1776.[32] It affirmed the doctrine of natural equality and inalienable rights in more explicit and unequivocal terms than even the Declaration of American Independence penned by the same hand. In neither case, however,

---

[30] Jefferson, *Reports*, 112, note by Jefferson. Possibly because servitude was now well exhausted as a system, it may have seemed more natural to say "person" for the imported one than "servant," no misunderstanding being foreseen. Its practical application probably did not extend beyond the ordinary imported persons, except possibly to a few Indians, though no case of this is on record.

[31] Hening, VII., 215; IX., 472.

[32] Hening, I., 47; X., 109. It affirmed, in the 1st, 4th, and 6th Articles of the Declaration, full equality before the law as to privileges, suffrage, life, liberty, property, and the pursuit of happiness.

would supreme authority, supported by a general public opinion, sustain the direct inference that negroes as men possessed the rights accorded to other men. The negative attitude of popular sentiment, supported by the courts, was a proof either of the sentimental character of these vaunted clauses and of their use as a political justification of the American Revolution, or of the opinion that the negro was actually not a man in the full sense of that term. Negative sentiment, however, was not unanimous. No less a legal authority than George Wythe, a signer of the Declaration of Independence and Chancellor of the State of Virginia, had the courage of his convictions to the extent of laying down the rule that whenever one person claims to hold another in slavery, "*onus probandi* lies on the claimant," on the ground that freedom is the birthright of every human being. We may feel certain, too, that Jefferson in his detestation of the social and political effects of slavery would willingly have extended that liberty to the slave as a natural right which he afterwards attempted to secure for him as a privilege by emancipation. Though imbued as he was with the French theory of natural equality, we have no reason to doubt that he was on this point consistent with his declaration and ready to put it into practical effect if he had had the power. But the reasoning of Wythe and Jefferson went beyond that of their time. The Virginia Court of Appeals disclaimed the decree of the Chancellor as far as it related "to native Africans and their descendants" who had been and were then held as slaves, but approved it as far as it related to whites and native American Indians. The proposition of the Court, though less humane, was more strictly legal than Wythe's. It refused properly, as it had no authority, to destroy the vested rights of property holders, which was a most probable consequence of Wythe's decision. But on the further point of the future enslavement of negroes it did not rule specifically, but by implication supported the principles of the Chancellor and of the Declaration of Rights.[33] It was in this particular but the mouthpiece of a general public sentiment that demanded the cessation of the slave trade, a sentiment that was now at last freed from the shackles imposed by colonial dependence upon England, and within two years was unanimous enough to demand prohibition in these words of the act of 1778 ; "No slave or slaves shall hereafter be imported into this common-wealth by sea or land, nor shall any slaves so imported be sold or bought by any person whatsoever."[34] The penalty attached to this law was, that slaves so imported should become free.[35]

The intent of prohibition was so genuine that persons taking up subsequent residence in the State were forced to make oath that none of the slaves brought with them had been imported from Africa or the West Indies since November 1, 1778, and that being the case, that further they had not brought this property with intent of transferring its ownership by bargain and sale. The only rights in slaves recognized by the act, therefore, were those of property interests already vested at the time of the passage of the act in citizens of Virginia, or in such citizens of the rest of the United States as might remove to Virginia as residents, and in the successors by descent, devise, or marriage of the legal owners of slaves. Travellers even were required to show that any slaves accompanying them were necessary personal attendants who would be removed with them.[36]

After this time no one could legally be held as a slave who was not so on the 1st of November, 1778, or the descendant of such a slave in the female line. This was an immediate inference from the negative legislation just cited, but, to pre-

---

[33] Hening & Munford, I., 134, 143, Hudgens *vs.* Wright; Hurd, *Law of Freedom and Bondage,* I., 246, note.

[34] Statutes of Virginia, 1778, 3rd. Sess., c. 1.

[35] It excepted those already vested by laws of other states.

[36] Hening, IX., 472.

vent mistakes, a bill stating the positive side of this declaration was framed and reported by the Revolutionary committee of revisors to the legislature of 1779,[37] and was finally enacted as a law in 1785.[38] Reënacted in the revisal of 1792, this law remained the legal basis of the designation of the slave without modification until 1860. In 1856, under the peculiar political stress of the time, the menace of the free negro element and sectional agitation, a way was opened for the voluntary enslavement of free negroes. This was by petition to the courts on the part of the negro, designating the master he wished to serve, who on his part had to give security and pay into court one-half the valuation of such a slave. Few negroes probably availed themselves of this privilege. A more efficacious method was provided during the legislative session of 1859–60, by authorizing the sale of free negroes convicted of penitentiary offenses into absolute slavery.[39] Both these acts were probably retaliatory and punitory, and had little practical effect. They but witness the extremity to which the free negro question that baffled Jefferson, Tucker, Randolph and the humanitarians of Virginia had driven the irritated and indignant majority.

The fourth and final step in the logical adoption of race as a full and sufficient criterion upon which to base dependent slavery is to be seen in a long series of earlier statutes that first drew and applied the color line as a limit upon various social and political rights, and finally narrowed its application definitely to the negro race with respect to liberty and customary or legal privileges and rights. The historic definition of this color line discrimination which has exerted such a potent influence on the disabilities of the negro—slave or freeman—is most interesting. Its earliest application was, as its latest has been, connected only with the negro race; but at

---

[37] Hening, IX., 472.

[38] *Ibid.*, preface vol. XII.; XII., 182, margin.

[39] Acts, 1856, c. 46; 1859–60, c. 54, see note.

various times it was applied to Indians, to Moors, to Moham-medans, and even, strange as it may now appear, to Jews. In the first instance it was purely social in intent and was designed to prevent race mixture. Thus, as early as 1630 and 1640, two white men, Hugh Davis and Robert Sweet, were the one "bound and whipped before an assembly of negroes and others" and the other made to do public penance in church for the offense of "lying with a negro," [40] when like offenses with whites were lightly punished, if at all. In fact the fornication of "Englishmen" with negro women was the direct cause of the act of 1662 that enunciated the doctrine of *partus sequitur ventrem*, which, imposing the mother's status upon the offspring, was expected to act as a deterrent influence upon the female. The guilty white was at the same time compelled to pay a fine of 1000 pounds of tobacco, double the amount exacted in other cases of fornication.[41] By the provisions of the act of 1662, which for the first time took cognizance of importations of this hybrid offspring into the colony as servants, such servants were reduced to slavery equally as if they were full blooded negroes or Indians. Any-thing that might enlarge this class of half breeds was strongly discountenanced. Intermarriage of a free white with a negro, mulatto or Indian, whether bond or free, was in 1691 made punishable with perpetual banishment of the white, and the offense of giving birth to a mulatto bastard was treated with far greater severity than was the case with white bastards.[42] The temporary servitude of the bastard itself was also pro-

---

[40] Hening, I., 146, 552. The negro woman was whipped in the latter case. Compare, *Ibid.*, pp. 145, 551, where in the case of fornication with whites the offense is not harshly dealt with. In 1657 it disbarred the offender from holding office or bearing witness; cf. also *Ibid.*, I., 252, 433.

[41] Hening, II., 115. A penalty of 500 pounds of tobacco was imposed in such cases by a law of 1661.

[42] Hening, III., 87, 453. If a free white woman offended she was fined £15, or sold into service for five years. If a servant white woman five years were added to her term.

vided for and, even if of free status by birth, it was bound out to service for thirty years.[43] In the revisal of 1705 the punishment for these offenses was made either more severe or more certain. A year of service was added to the penalty in the case of women servants, and in the case of the marriage of free whites with persons of the colored classes six months imprisonment without bail and a fine of £10 was substituted for banishment, as this penalty had been found inoperative because the duty of execution had been left in the hands of the county justices but not the means of enforcing it.[44] A minister or other person who should perform such a marriage was subjected to a fine of 10,000 pounds of tobacco, half of which was to go to the informer. This was certainly the most efficacious mode of combatting the evil, as it practically shut up the avenue to legal or secret marriage, though it could not do so to concubinage.

In the recognized impossibility of completely checking the growth of a mulatto class the only alternative left was to reduce this class as far as possible to the status of the lower parent, so we find that as long as a trace of the inferior blood was commonly recognizable the person was socially, as well as legally, treated as far as possible as a full blooded Indian or negro. Thus mulattoes, like negroes and Indians, could not hold office nor could they bear witness except against persons of their color. Nor could they, even though free, hold in servitude any one except those "of their own complexion." This disability also applied to Jews, Moors and Mohammedans.[45] Blood was supposed to be traceable in the negro at least two generations farther than in the case of the Indians, so in the earliest legal definition of the mulatto class, *i. e.*; in

---

[43] This was punitory, and intended to restrain such offenses as well as to save the parish the cost of maintaining the bastard.

[44] Hening, III., 453, 456.

[45] Hening, III., 252, 293; 1705, c. 49; III., 88. A mulatto slave if freed, like the negro, had to be transported out of the colony.

the disabling act of 1705, where negroes, Indians, and mulattoes are classed with criminals, the terms were held to embrace only the children of Indians, but the children, grandchildren and great grandchildren of negroes. The discrimination against the negro mulatto if not based upon complexion, is at least historically explicable. In the early days no great antipathy was exhibited against amalgamation with the Indians. Though it never reached the extent with the English that it did with the French colonists, numerous instances of intermarriage are recorded. The noted example of Pocahontas and Rolfe may be exceptional from the possible political interests involved in this semi-royal and diplomatic marriage, but the Spanish ambassador in London, Zuñiga, in a letter to Philip of Spain cites with some interest twenty such marriages in Virginia, and represents it as an advocated policy.[46] Beyond the second degree of the Indian and the fourth of the negro mulatto, there was no bar but sentiment to prevent miscegenation, and if we can believe the Huguenot, Peter Fontain, sentiment as late as 1757 was not a sufficient barrier even against the negro descendants of the fourth generation. Actual marriage with whites did take place, he states, and worse still, that the country swarmed with mulatto bastards.[47]

Mulatto bastards, who by law were obliged to serve some master until thirty-one years of age, were themselves a fertile source of a new bastard element. Their position rendered them especially eligible for gross purposes, both in their intimate contact with the negroes and in their relations to their employers. The law had unwittingly set a premium upon immorality, as the fall of the female mulatto not only added an additional term to her period of service, but her offspring was by a law of 1723 in its turn forced to serve the master until the age of thirty-one years. Such mulatto servants, then, were scarcely better off as to prospective freedom than

---

[46] Brown, *Genesis of United States*, Letters of Zuñiga, 572, 632.
[47] Fontaine, *Huguenot Family*, 350.

the negro slave. Custom tended to reduce them to a state of actual slavery. About the middle of the eighteenth century (*circa* 1765) the practice arose of actually disposing of their persons by sale, both in the colony and without, as slaves. So flagrant was the practice that further legislation was demanded to check the illegal proceeding by appropriate penalties.[48] It would appear that the offenders were those who were entitled to the mulattoes only as servants, but used the power of their possession for intimidation or deceit, which could be easily practiced in the case of minor bastards born in their service. For this reason, and probably as an additional protection, the period of service was at this time greatly lessened, as "an unreasonable severity" upon children, to twenty-four years for males and eighteen years for females, whether the child were the bastard of a free white, or of a servant, white or colored.[49] The practice was probably not wholly checked, for as late as 1788 it was discovered that the offense existed of kidnapping the children of free blacks and mulattoes and disposing of them as slaves. This was made punishable by death without benefit of clergy, as the Assembly thought "a punishment adequate to such crimes" had not been hitherto provided.[50] Fear of capital punishment, however, was not strong enough to restrain the greed of some slave dealers. A case occurred in 1791 which was notorious for the escape of the criminal on a technical point of law. Probably to prevent a similar occurrence the law of 1798 covering the point was enacted.

The mulatto was finally and more strictly defined in a Revolutionary bill of 1779, which was enacted in 1785 and became a law in 1787. Any person one of whose grandparents had been a negro, though all of his progenitors,

---

[48] Hening, VIII., 133, 134. The seller forfeited to the buyer £15 over the amount of the purchase money and £20 to the informer. For a second offense he lost the service of the servant.

[49] Hening, VIII., 134, 135.          [50] Hening, XII., 531.

except that one, and his descendants were white, and every one who had one-fourth part or more of negro blood was deemed a mulatto.[51] This law, which extended the contamination of blood only to the third generation and to the quadroon as a final limit, disregarded Indian mulattoes entirely, and is evidence that they had practically ceased to exist. It is an important law both for its mitigating influence as compared with the laws of some other States, and because it became the basis of similar legislation in several States, notably Kentucky, Arkansas and Illinois, and remained in force until the complete close of the slave *régime* in Virginia.[52] The law henceforth made no practical discrimination between the negro and the mulatto, and the courts in 1849 confirmed the principle that "negro" in any statute should be construed to include "mulatto as well as negro."[53] Virginia law and custom never distinguished the separate mestizo or "mustee" class so common in the Carolinas. This was the joint offspring of the negro and Indian, and in the Carolinas was subject to the same disabilities as the negro and mulatto.[54] The earlier extinction of the Indian in Virginia and the practical close of Indian slavery before any large numbers of Indians and negroes had been brought together probably explain this fact.

In the North the sanctity and purity of white blood was guarded by similar legislation. Mulattoes were a well-defined

---

[51]Hening, XII., 184.

[52] See the Virginia Law of 1865; cf. Illinois Session Laws, 1827, January 6; Arkansas Laws, 1843, January 20; Kentucky Revised Statutes, 1852, sec. 7. In North Carolina a law of 1723 included the third generation, and the law of 1826 included the fourth generation. (North Carolina Laws, 1723, c. 5; Revised Statutes, North Carolina, 1826, c. 21.) The Tennessee Law (1794, c. 1., sec. 32) included the third generation, and in Ohio (1849) the uncertain criterion of 'nearer black than white' was employed. This was also the case in South Carolina, the determination being left to the jury, whose range of discretion lay between the octoroon and quadroon. De Bow, *Resources*, Vol. 11., p. 270.

[53] Grattan, *Reports*, XI., 484, 541.

[54] De Bow, *Resources*, II., 271; South Carolina Statutes, v. 8, 352; Laws, 1792; North Carolina Laws, 1723, c. 5.

class in Connecticut by 1690 and in Massachusetts by 1698, and were treated in law as Indians or negroes. Restraining acts to prevent a "spurious and mixt issue" as early as 1705 and 1708 ordered the sale of offending negroes and mulattoes out of the colony's jurisdiction, and punished Christians who intermarried with them by a fine of £50. As late as 1786 in Massachusetts such marriages were declared void and the £50 penalty was still exacted, and not until 1843 was this act repealed. Thus was the color line, with its social and legal distinctions, extended beyond the conditions of servitude and slavery to freemen, in the spirit of the Virginia statute of 1668, which declared, "though permitted to enjoy their freedom, yet [the enfranchised] ought not in all respects to be admitted to a full fruition of the exemptions and immunities of the English." [55]

The most important disabilities incident to slavery came as a result of the developed conception of property in the person rather than in his service, which tended completely to confound and identify the *person* of the slave with the *thing* owned. The property idea inherited from servitude had reached a limited conception of personality which conferred upon the master certain rights incidental to such a chattel estate, at the same time that it subjected it to the rules at law governing chattels personal. This conception involved not merely legal forms, but important disabilities as to both the servant and the slave. Thus the right of (1) *alienation*, either by will or *inter vivos*, was both a cause and a consequence of the property conception. It included transfer of the whole or part of the subject's obligations, for valuable or other consideration, to other persons and places even beyond the jurisdiction of the State. So also the disability of (2) *seizure*, involving alienation, was a liability of the servant and of the slave as of other visible property to be taken by execution for the satisfaction

[55] Moore, *Slavery*, 52, 54, 59; Massachusetts Statutes, 1786, June 22, c. 3; 1705, c. 4; Hening, II., 267.

of debt. Other legal results were the specific valuation and rating of servants and slaves as personal assets in inventories and appraisements of estates, and the fact that they passed with the personalty to the executors or administrators, and not to the heirs at law, of intestates.

By the time of the codification of 1705 it was found necessary to advance the property notion of the slave from personalty to realty for the sake of justice to owners and heirs in settling and preserving estates. The change was almost wholly for legal purposes, and in only a few instances hardened or extended the incidents of personalty inherited by slavery from servitude. Had the conception of realty been made complete it would have tended to modify for the better the condition of the slave somewhat in the same manner as the territorial element in feudalism acted to mitigate the personal servitude of the English and French villain by restricting alienation, particularly devise.[56] The chief object of the act was to protect orphans, widows and reversioners in their rights by saving widow's dowers, and preventing a defeat of reversionary interests by a widow or widow's husband selling dower slaves out of the colony. Slaves descended now not as movables but as fee simple land of inheritance to the heirs and widows. Dower was first set aside and the rest of the intestate estate inventoried, appraised, and given to the heir at law to divide equally amongst the children. It was here that the incident of (3) *separation* of families, also involved in alienation, was made capable of extension until checked by law. This was finally done in 1801 by a decree of the Supreme Court of Appeals which declared that "an equal division of slaves in number and value is not always possible and is sometimes improper when it cannot be exactly done without separating infant children from their mothers, which humanity forbids and will not be countenanced in a court of equity, so that a compensation for the excess must in

---

[56] Vinogradoff, *Villainage*, 76; Hening, III., 333–335, 371.

such cases be made and received in money." [57]   The right to separate husband and wife, and larger children, however, still remained.   Even before the law of 1705 the courts had attempted to check the growth of this incident through the right of devise of chattels.   Devises of children, particularly of children not *in esse* at the testator's death (devises adjudged void), were declared by the general court in 1695 to be neither "convenient nor humanitarian," as the owner of the mother would not be careful of her in pregnancy nor of the child when born, "and many children might hence die; and besides," said the court, "it was an unreasonable charge" without benefit to the owner of the mother.   Such cases, however, of devise of increase continued to come into court for judgment or to force compromise.[58]

Important legal and equitable results followed the conception of the slave as real estate.   Rights varying in respect to their duration or to the time of their enjoyment were created, and the various freehold estates, such as estates tail (general and special, male and female); estates for life, and *pur autre vie*, dower, courtesy, and estates upon condition, as mortgage; and estates less than freehold; as well as rights not only in possession but in reversion and remainder; and rights not at common law, such as uses, were recognized.   Slaves were brought within the provisions of the English Statute of Uses, and together with lands might be conveyed to uses.   Trusts, however, often operated to mitigate their condition in restricting alienation. {The object of entails was social and economic, that slaves might pass to the same persons as lands and tenements and furnish them the necessary means for the improvement of them at the same time that the integrity of estates was assured.{   As difference of opinion existed as to the validity of entails where slaves were not specifically annexed to lands,

---

[57] Call, *Reports*, III., 17, 52, 53.   Fitzhugh *et ux. vs.* Foote; Stone *vs.* Pope *et al.*

[58] Jefferson, *Reports*, 40, 43, 47.

this mode was prescribed by a law of 1727 covering the transfer of estates, " tail, in possession or remainder," with annexed " slaves, or their increase," saving only that creditor's rights were protected in the continued liability of this property for debts. This developed a new incident, (4) *annexation,* which operated in a manner not unlike that ascribed to the principle *regardant* in villainage, designed to tie the slaves to the land. The modes of the acquisition of title to realty which included forfeitures as well as succession, or devolution, and alienation by will, deed, marriage, bargain and sale were now applicable to slaves. Forfeiture, however, only occurred where the land and tenements of the person might be forfeited.

The legal effects of the act of 1705 were at first regarded as beneficial, particularly in the security offered to the estates of orphans whose parents died intestate, but such various constructions, contrary judgments, and opinions involving controversy and litigation arose that in 1727 it was necessary to pass an explanatory act amending some of the earlier provisions. In 1705 slaves had been specifically left as personalty in several important particulars. As chattels they were still liable to be taken in execution for debt; they did not escheat but went as other personalty; were recoverable by personal action for detainer, trover, or conversion ; their ownership did not confer, as that of real estate, the franchise ; and it was not essential that their transfer be recorded, as was necessary in the alienation of realty. This last point gave rise to a dispute as to whether it was confined to sale, money payment, and transmutation of possession without writing, or whether it extended to alienation by deed, will, and marriage which need not be recorded. The act of 1727 settled the issue by recognizing the chattel character of the slave as to alienation by vesting the slaves of the wife absolutely in the husband, and by passing the absolute interest by bargain and sale, gift with or without deed, or by will written or non cupative in the manner of personalty ; and henceforth remainders could be limited only as those of chattels personal by rules of common

5

law. The act further secured the rights of widows and mino
orphans by substituting equitable for legal procedure in
recovering dower or forcing partition. This in 1705 had been
hampered by the tedious real actions, writ of dower and wri
of partition, not so well adapted to living things as a bill in
equity, and by allowing a widow dissatisfied with her hus
band's will to renounce its provisions and claim her dower
and by exempting slaves from seizure if other personalty
existed to satisfy debts.[59]

The legislation outlined established such a mixed property
conception of slaves, making them, in the words of the Assembly, "real estate in some respects, personal in others, and both
in others," that it resulted in much legal confusion and litigation, destroying and creating titles, involving frequent suits
and all manner of doubts and varieties of conflicting opinions
as new and undetermined points constantly arose. Such unfortunate and unexpected results, defeating the real ends of
the enactments, led to an attempt on the part of the revisors
of 1748 to repeal these laws and enact others returning to the
earlier conception of the slave as a chattel personal, which they
regarded not only as simpler and more beneficial but as the
natural conception of the slave as a movable. This would
have enabled children to share with the elder brother in the
slaves of intestate collaterals and would have stopped annexa-
tions for entailment, which had bad practical effects. Just as
the principle "*regardant* to a manor," as Vinogradoff has
shown, did not mitigate the condition of the English villain
by giving him rights against the lord to prevent his being

---

[59] Hening, IV., 227, 228; V., 37, 443, 445. By 1738 sheriffs upon writs
of *fieri facias* and collectors of officers' fees and levies, in making distress
had done so much damage in seizing slaves of greater value than the debt
that they were hereafter for such executions limited to £10 or over in value
where other personalty was visible. In England the Court of Chancery
gradually assumed jurisdiction in enforcing partition similarly in joint
tenancy upon a bill filed in equity, and these writs were abolished in
1833–34. Statutes, 3 and 4, Will., IV., c. 27, 536.

shifted from place to place or from predial to other labor, as was the case with the *colonus*, the villain of the later Roman Empire, who was *ascriptus glebae*, a part and parcel of the estate, and could not quit the land—so the principle of annexation failed to bring any beneficial effect to the slave. He and his increase were not kept upon the land with which by will or deed they were legally bound up in title, but were transferred for economic reasons to other lands of the master in different counties or parts of the colony far away from any record of their annexation, which ultimately might be wholly lost sight of. This practice in the absence of genealogical registers often confused fee simple with entailed slaves of the same name and sex, deceiving purchasers and creditors and destroying foreign credit, upon which the whole trade system of Virginia depended.[60] While, on the contrary, if the slaves were kept on the lands to which they were annexed their increase soon so overstocked the plantation as to inflict an unreasonable damage on the tenant in tail. And as such slaves were liable to be taken in execution and sold for debt, the sale acting to bar the entail, it encouraged unscrupulous mesne tenants to borrow money, run into debt, and sacrifice the slaves in payment, so defeating their settlement.

For these and other legal reasons, as well as to keep estates together by allowing the heir to an intestate's land to buy the slaves of the other children at appraised values, and by limiting the widow's allowance to a life estate in the third part of an intestate's slaves to guard against dispersion by second marriage, two substitute acts were passed in the revisal of 1748, to go into effect June 10, 1751. These, as well as eight other laws passed at the same time, were repealed by the king's proclamation on October 31, 1751, but the repeal not being communicated to the Virginia Assembly until April 8, 1752, they had a limited duration and were printed with the

---

[60] Hening, V., 432–442; Vinogradoff, *Villainage*, 26, 55, 56; Sohm, *Roman Law*, 115.

other laws in 1752. The Assembly sent an urgent appeal to the king to revoke his repeal, but only two of the ten laws were suffered to receive the assent of Governor Dinwiddie in 1753.[61] One of them for the better government of servants and slaves summed up all the previous legislation still in effect except that relating to property, which had been repealed. But in this respect the condition of the slave remained substantially unchanged from 1727 to the end of the period of British domination, when in the first Republican Assembly, in the first year of the Commonwealth, Jefferson secured the passage of his bill abolishing entails, which made all donees in tail, present and future, owners of the fee simple estate in lands and slaves. This was designed as a vital blow to the perpetuity of a social aristocracy, and seems to have had a beneficial effect upon the slave as tenants in tail were disposed by interest to use slaves to their greatest advantage during possession without a proper regard for their care and future preservation which, however, was a motive that appealed to the owner of the fee simple estate.[62] The only important exception was a change necessitated by the frequent secret gifts of slaves for fraudulent purposes, the donor remaining in visible possession, by which creditors and purchasers were involved in expensive or unsuccessful lawsuits. By acts of 1757 and 1758 valid gifts could only be made by deed or will duly proven and recorded, and all verbal gifts had to be reduced to writing or possession delivered, else the gifts were void. It was not intended to make writing necessary where there was actual transmutation of possession to the donee, which was a common mode of gift. But an adju-

---

[61] Hening, V., 432–448 and note, 565; IV., 224; *Dinwiddie Papers*, I., 29, 30, 39.

[62] Hening, VI., 356; IX., 226; Ford, *Jefferson*, I., 49; II., 104, 105, 240. Pendleton opposed Jefferson for partial abolition, but the latter won by a few votes. He held it protected creditors, and the *morale* of young prospective tenants, and saved the valuable time of the legislature and money in defeating and docking entails.

·dication in the latter part of the century, having declared such gifts void, so disturbed titles that an act of 1787 was necessary to specially exempt from the acts gifts of donors who delivered possession to the donee, as they were in no sense fraudulent in intent nor deceptive in influence. Consequently the restriction of alienation involved was limited in its effect.·

A curious result of the conception of the slave as a subject of property was developed by the scarcity of specie in the years 1782 and 1783. Slaves and land were made to take the place of currency to relieve debtors as well as creditors. Slaves were declared legal tender in money judgments not exceeding £20, and in land judgments for sums not over £100. Like the laws of 1705 and 1793 [63] limiting the powers of officers of the law to make unreasonable seizures of slaves in execution for debt, a law was passed in 1792 exempting them from distraint by the sheriff and tax collectors if "other sufficient distress" could be had, or from such "unreasonable seizures or distresses" as would render them liable to the action of the party grieved. But if other property were not available a creditor might seize even emancipated slaves, though they had enjoyed-their freedom for many years, as any other rule would have caused emancipation in order to defeat creditors. In estates less than freehold, as the leasing and hiring of slaves was common, cases often arose where the tenant or successor to the greater or less estate might suffer considerable damage. In the case of a lease of slaves from a life tenant, for instance, and his death after the first of March, the lessee was to hold the slaves till the first of December of the following year, paying for the time, and delivering them well clothed. [64]

The complicated cases and results arising from the conception of the slave as both realty and personalty in the acts of legislation outlined were as troublesome and confusing to the

---

[63] Hening, VII., 118, 237; XI., 179, 349; XII., 505, 506; *Virginia Statutes at Large*, I., 47, 213.

[64] *Statutes at Large*, I., 98, 1792 act.; Call, *Reports*, IV., 336.

courts as to the legislature. Appeals from the lower courts were frequent, and dissenting opinions were constantly being delivered by the judges of the highest court, calling eventually for fresh statutory legislation to settle mooted points. The complexity of this mixed conception was not wholly cleared away even in its simplified form. Slaves were real estate as to descent, entails, and dower, and unlike chattels were protected from distress; but they were, like chattels real, not included in hereditaments as estates of inheritance, and also like chattels real survived to the survivor. In other respects also, they were personal estate; they were assets in the hands of the executor and liable for debt; they might be sold, sued for or taken in execution as chattels personal; they were inventoried and appraised and they did not escheat; wives' slaves were vested in their husbands; they could only be given or bequeathed as chattels, and no remainder other than that of a chattel personal at common law could be limited. The evident disposition of the courts in their decisions was to regard slaves as far as possible as personal estate, which was considered their natural condition.[65]

Probably no attempt by the legislature to return to the simple and earlier conception of slaves as personal estate would have succeeded during English domination, but not until a number of years after the commonwealth era was the change actually made by a law of 1792–93 reducing the several acts concerning slaves, free negroes, and mulattoes to one. This law saying, "All negro and mulatto slaves in all courts of judicature shall be held and adjudged to be personal estate," was the final step in defining the conception of the slave as property, and in fixing his resulting disabilities Dower, strictly speaking, could not now exist, and was converted into a use for life of such slaves as fell to a widow's

---

[65] Hening, V., 440, note; Jefferson, *Reports*, 1, 5, 37, 125; Washington *Reports*, II., 1–7; Call, *Reports*, II., 473; Ball *vs.* Ball, Munford, *Reports* III., 283; *Ibid.*, II., 501.

share, which use upon marriage was disposed of to the husband, just as a wife's interest in personalty was vested in the husband and his representatives.

The most important corollary of the general conception of property in the slave was that as a subject of property, as a subject of rights, he could legally neither own nor enjoy property in his own right. This added a distinct disability to his legal status in abridging the civil right of (5) *private property.* A limited property right, not unlike the Roman *peculium*, was allowed the slave by custom, though not by law. Masters frequently gave them horses, cattle or hogs for free disposal in their own right, and the negro servants reduced to slavery in 1661 doubtless were possessed of property. This right was taken away by a law of 1692, which converted such property to the use of the master, and, upon his neglect to appropriate it, it was to be forfeited to the parish for the support of the poor. The custom, however, of masters assigning to slaves such property for management as *peculium* continued in spite of the law, and extended even to small tracts of land.[66]

Had the conception of property in the slave been absolute it would have wholly divested him of the other civil rights of personal security and personal liberty, as it did of all political capacity, but the fact of natural personalty with which the slave was actually endowed was not lost sight of, and limited the effect of the property notion to creating certain civil disabilities rather than a total abrogation of rights. Thus (6) *disfranchisement*, (7) *incapacity for office*, and (8) *juridical incapacity* after 1732, except in suits for freedom, were regarded as incident to the condition of slave, while a servant and a free person of color, if a freeholder, had a limited enjoyment of public rights in the franchise and the ability to maintain a suit and to bear witness legally. The disabilities of the slave extended even into the domain of private rights. He

---

[66] Hening, III., 103, 460.

was denied (9) *marriage* and (10) *trade*, because as property he could not choose nor make a contract.[67]

The law did in some respects regard slaves as a distinct class of persons, and from this conception and its limitation important incidental rights and duties followed as the master gradually acquired power over their minds and bodies as well as over their service. As persons, like male whites and Indian servants of sixteen years of age, and free negroes, all slaves, male and female, were tithables after March, 1661, the master of course paying the levy. This liability, which was retained upon free negro females up to 1769, was inherited from servitude. By the acts of 1779 and 1781 slaves were still liable to a poll tax, of £5 and of 10 s. respectively, to be paid by the owner. The court of chancery also recognized the personality of the slave by permitting persons holding a legal estate in slaves to sue in equity, although a remedy at law existed. Slaves were held to be not property only, but " rational beings and entitled to the humanity of the court," which in decisions took into consideration the mutual attachment of master and slave and its value, which was not recognized by a jury. The chancellor often protected freedmen from sale under a creditor's execution, and would even enforce a contract between master and slave which had been wholly or in part complied with on the part of the slave. The common law courts, however, refused to recognize the contractural ability of the slave and might reverse any such

---

[67] Hening, III., 252, 298; IV., 134, 327; XII., 182; *Virginia Reports,* Randolph, VI., 173; Leigh, I., 172; Grattan, XIV., 193. Free negroes, mulattoes, and Indians were disfranchised in 1723 owing to insurrectionary troubles. In 1732, like slaves, they could only bear witness in the trial of a slave for a capital offense, and by the law of 1785 they could only witness in pleas of the commonwealth against negroes or mulattoes. By the code of 1705 negroes, mulattoes, and Indians, like convicts of crime, could hold no office ecclesiastical, civil, or military, or any place of public trust or power under penalty of a fine of 500 pounds of tobacco, and 20 pounds per month during tenure. Together with popish recusants and non-Christians they were also wholly incapacitated from bearing witness.

decision.[68] In equity, however, the slave might maintain his suit for freedom on (11) the *contractural power* recognized by his master to that end. Masters even went into business agreements with slaves granting them the license required by law for freedom of movement and the private right of trade in consideration of a stipulated payment to be made by the slave. The slave hired himself to other masters or otherwise acted as a freeman. As this became in time a public nuisance from the premium it set upon theft and unlawful practices on the part of slaves forced to meet their obligations, it was restricted in 1769 under penalty of a forfeit of £10 from the master for every such license.

The law also recognized (12) the *personal agency* of the slave and held him personally responsible for independent action, except where it was shown that he acted under order of his superior, master or overseer. This is shown particularly in the course of penal legislation. In perjury, for instance, the slave with the negro and mulatto suffered in his own person in the pillory, maiming, and whipping in lieu of fine and imprisonment.[69] The slave retained like the free negro and mulatto his capacity as (13) *witness.* This was restricted by an act of 1732 to the criminal courts, to trials of slaves for capital offenses, where negro evidence was often of value. In 1800 the right was extended to include free negroes as well as criminal slaves. The personality of the slave as well as of the servant was again recognized in his specific exemption with certain other persons from (14) *militia service,* the exemp-

---

[68] Hening, I., 306, 329, 356, 361, 454; II., 84, 296, 486; IV., 133; VIII., 393; X., 12, 504; *Virginia Reports,* Munford, III., 570; Leigh, I., 73, 465.

[69] Hening, III., 451, 463; IV., 27; Revised Code, 1808; II., 147; Hening and Munford, *Reports,* II., 6. He was punished by whipping when no one would go his bond for the fine imposed. See "Killing deer out of season," 1705; "Hog stealing," etc. For a second offence in hog stealing whites suffered like negroes in the pillory, and had their ears cut off. For a third offence whites and blacks alike were adjudged felons and punishable with death.

tion being based upon his obligations toward his master and the danger of putting arms into his hands. Thus also, when free negroes, mulattoes, and Indians were enlisted it was only for servile duties. Slaves were, however, employed both in the Revolutionary War and in the War of Secession. For their conspicuous service in the former many gained their freedom, and the project of raising a slave army by the reward of eventual freedom was advocated and adopted by the Confederate Congress only too late to become an important weapon in the struggle. By an act of 1862, the Governor of Virginia was authorized, on the call of the President of the Confederacy, to use as many as 10,000 slaves for sixty days' service on fortifications or defense.[70] As a person, also, the slave had, by a law of 1723, the right of (15) *notification* of disabilities. This right presupposed the ability of choice and an independent will contrary to the strict Roman conception of a slave. The legal mode of notification prescribed was two-fold, (1) by the parish church wardens, who read the act twice a year, in April and October, from a registered copy, in every church and chapel publicly after worship, and (2) by the sheriffs of each county yearly at the county court, proclaiming it from the court-house door. Both officials were put under heavy penalty for the faithful discharge of their duty, which was important alike to master and to slave.[71]

The personal liberty allowed by custom on holidays and free time, like Sundays, was not restricted by law until 1680, when it became a social necessity to do so on account of the rapid growth of slave population and the danger of plots and

---

[70] Hening, III., 336; IV., 327; V., 245, 546; VI., 533; XI., 414; Statutes, 1800, 3, 43; 1862, October 21; 1863, p. 42. In 1764 this restriction on bearing witness was removed from free negroes, mulattoes, and Indians, and they were allowed the right in all cases, civil as well as criminal, against their color. In 1863 the number of slaves liable to military service was changed to 5 per cent. In such cases the master received remuneration.

[71] Hening, IV., 134.

insurrections if slaves, speaking their native tongue, unintelligible to the whites, were allowed freely to congregate and visit. Hitherto they had been allowed to assemble freely at feasts and burials as was their custom, and to absent themselves from their masters' plantations. Now the right of (16) *free movement* was limited upon certificate from his superior, master or overseer, which could only be given upon special and necessary occasions. Without this the slave could not absent himself from his owner's plantation nor could he carry any weapon, offensive or defensive. This was made to apply also to marriage and trade which, were allowed within limits, when duly sanctioned by the master, who thereby assumed any civil liabilities that might arise. No legal marriage could be made between whites and negroes, however sanctioned, but a slave so marrying was not liable to punishment, while the white persons and their abettors were. This is a case where the law discriminated against the white in favor of the slave. The same was true in the case of persons dealing with slaves who had not their superior's license to trade. The slave went unpunished as in the other case, on the presumption that he was under undue influence, but the other party was liable criminally and civilly. He suffered fine or imprisonment or both, or corporal punishment, or damages equal to four times the value of the article bought.[72]

The slave was also protected in a limited enjoyment of his right of (17) *personal security.* The duty of protection, as in feudalism and in patriarchal slavery, was a recognized obligation of the master, who stood between his dependent and third parties. The law further intervened to guarantee protection. Maiming a slave was as much a penitentiary offense as maiming a free man. Such was the unanimous decision of the General Court on the terms of the act of 1803, which, it was declared, protected both alike. A second case coming into

---

[71] Hening, III., 451, 452; VI., 360; XII., 283; *Statutes at Large* n. s., II., 329. For dealing on the Sabbath $10 additional was exacted.

the court in 1827 was dealt with in the same way on the basis of the law of 1819, and the offender was declared a felon. Strangers had no authority over slaves except what was assigned by the master.   So, when slaves were hired or bound out by covenant or loaned, conditions were attached that they were to be treated in a "lawful and humane manner," and specification was also made as to the kind of employment, which was not to be hazardous.   Even if such stipulations were not attached to the instrument, they might be assumed, as the bailee was not regarded as vested with the full rights of the master.[73]

Connected with this, in protection both of the master's property and the slaves' personal rights, the offense of slave stealing was subjected to extreme punishment as a crime.   A law of 1798 inflicted the penalty of death without benefit of clergy upon the thief, but after the construction of a penitentiary this was commuted to imprisonment from 3 to 8 years. Because of the refusal of other jurisdictions to recognize principles of extradition, however, it was impossible wholly to prevent the offense.   An interesting case arose in 1839, where two men attached to a New York schooner stole a Virginia slave, and a requisition for them was refused by Governor William H. Seward, of New York, on the ground that they had not committed treason or felony within the provisions of the United States Constitution, which did not embrace State laws ; that there was no such crime as slave stealing in common law, as slavery was not so recognized ; that New York had abolished slavery and the offense was a crime only by statute law of Virginia.   For this action the Governor was accused by several New York and Massachusetts papers of having infringed not only a precedent of one of his predecessors in office but also a decision of the Supreme Court of New York, and of violating a provision of the United States Constitution.

---

[73] Grattan, *Reports*, XV., 410;  *Virginia Cases*, I., 184;  Randolph *Reports*, V., 661, m. 3, 350; 5, 305, 483, 485; Leigh, *Reports*, VIII., 566.

Another process by which like results might be accomplished was the secret transportation of slaves out of the colony by third parties. The license of the master or the certificate or pass of public authorities, secretary, or clerk of the county court was necessary in 1705 to free the transporter from a penalty of £100. Masters of vessels clearing port had to make search and give oath that they carried no such slaves. Transportation was not always a disadvantage to the slave. Many negro slaves escaped on certificates of registry lent them by free blacks, and this, because ship masters abetted, became an important illegal means of enfranchisement, even in the eighteenth century. In 1805 the master's consent was requisite for transportation even beyond the limits of the county or corporation, and breach of the law was a misdemeanor punishable by a fine of from $100 to $500 and imprisonment for from two to four years, together with civil liability for the value of the slave. This latter feature was afterwards extended to the operations of railway companies.[74]

The most grievous incidents of the condition of slavery were a direct consequence of the penal legislation essential to protect the master in his rights and to ensure peace and security in the community. This development was the inevitable result of irresponsible and unregulated action in the slave's own person, and in general it applied only to the criminal classes. The property right of the master involved control over the slave's person and power of regulating his conduct where it was reprehensible. The means employed for this purpose was in the nature of a paternal right and was common both to English servitude, villainage and apprenticeship, and American indentured servitude. Developed as an incident of servitude, (18) *corporal punishment* was retained when this status passed into that of slavery. Humanity and

---

[74] *Virginia Cases,* 14 (June 26, 1792); *Statutes at Large, United States,* II., 78, 148, 450 note; III., 123; *Richmond Enquirer,* January 12, 1840; Hening, III., 270, 273; IV., 173–175; IX., 187; *Statutes at Large,* 1819, 432.

self interest were at first supposed to be sufficient motives to limit the extent of this power of the master to its rational use, but when they failed to do so the law intervened. As a penalty inflicted by the State for certain offenses ; such as lifting his hand against a Christian white, keeping arms or dogs, running away, absenting himself, and various offenses within clergy, it was limited to from twenty to thirty-nine lashes. It was presumed with this example that masters would not exceed the maximum, but where they did so without inflicting serious personal injury the slave had no legal remedy. He was protected, however, against his master, as well as against third persons, in his right to (19) *life and limb*, but this right was abridged in the case of obstinate slaves resisting their masters' correction, as violent means seemed necessary to control them. By an act of 1669, if such a resisting slave was casually killed in consequence of correction it was not a felony, and the master was "aquit of molestation," said the law, "since it cannot be presumed that prepensed malice (which alone makes murther ffelony) should induce any man to destroy his own estate." The prevalence and danger to society of absconding slaves led to an extension of this abridgment in 1672. Prior to this, runaway servants and slaves had been treated precisely alike, but now a number of negroes being in rebellion and evading suppression it was made lawful for any one attempting to capture runaways by warrant or hue and cry to wound or even kill absconding slaves that resisted arrest. This law was continued in 1680, 1691, and 1701 from fear of insurrection, theft, and arson. It applied to runaway slaves lying hid and committing depredations who resisted lawful arrest, and the act was to be published every six months in the counties and parishes to serve as a deterrent influence. In 1701 a notorious slave, Billy, who for a number of years had avoided arrest, terrorizing the counties of James City, York, and New Kent by his robberies and threats, was attainted and a price set upon his head of 1,000 pounds of tobacco.[75]   By the code of 1705 outlying slaves who refused to heed the proclamation of the county justice published at the door of every church and chapel of the county on Sunday, warning them to return to their masters, were outlawed and liable to be killed or captured by any person, without warrant or further accusation.   If the master chose to apply to the county court to punish the outlawed slave when apprehended, it was in its discretion to order punishment "by dismembering or any other way not touching his life for the reclaiming of any such incorrigible slave and terrifying others from the like practice."

The menace to life and property from a number of sources was so real in the late years of the seventeenth and early years of the eighteenth centuries that it is not surprising to find the growing rigor of general penal legislation reflected in the treatment of criminal slaves.   Militia and garrisons had to be kept in constant readiness in fear of the Indian outbreaks. People went to church under arms.   Rebellion against the constituted authorities was rife, and even divine service was not sacred from "unseemly and indecent" interruptions.   An intended insurrection of negroes discovered in the Northern Neck in 1687 particularly alarmed the colonists, as the negro population at this time was about equal to that of the whites, and the unruly convict and " spirited " class of white servants, which had for many years been giving trouble, were equally dangerous.   Duties had no appreciable effect in checking the importations of slaves, which after 1685 showed alarming increase, and intended insurrections were discovered in 1710, 1722, and in 1730.

Practically little distinction was made between habitual runaway servants and slaves.[76]   Slaves were included in the acts

---

[75] Hening, II., 270, 299, 481; III., 86, 210, 457, 459; IV., 169; VI., 295; *Revised Code.*, 1819, II., 288.

[76] Hening, II., 483, 484, 493, 562; III., 87, 456, 461; IV., 170, 171; Burk, *Virginia*, II., 300; Ballagh, *White Servitude*, 60; cf. the Gloucester Plot of 1663, *idem*, 92.

against runaway servants after 1670 and were pursued, captured, and punished in the same way.   They were whipped to
the same extent as servants, and were, like them, if unclaimed,
imprisoned or hired out to work with an iron collar on their
necks stamped " P. G." (public gaol) for their identification,
and were branded as runaways with the letter " R."   But
unlike the servant, the slave was not liable to his master for
damages in addition to punishment.   The damage sustained
on account of the slave was paid by the servant in whose
company he ran away.   In the earlier days fugitive slaves did
not generally go out of the jurisdiction of Virginia, but
escaped to the swamps, the woods on the frontiers, or the
Eastern Shore, where they remained a constant menace as to
depredations and insurrectionary plots.   In this light, restriction of the personal liberty of the slave in the provisions
against bearing arms, and against assembling or absenting himself from the plantation without a pass, and the system of
espionage which grew up become clear.   Any one who allowed
a slave to remain over four hours on his property without such
a pass was liable to heavy financial penalties.   Actual or
incipient criminality also explains the provisions for preventing resistance to authority and assaults upon his superiors,
and the apparent harshness of the law of outlawry and of the
right of extreme corporal punishment assumed by the master.
As these conditions passed away, the law showed a tendency
to mitigate its rigor.   The discretionary right of dismemberment was taken away from the county court in 1769 as
" barbarous," and the power of two justices to outlaw was
repealed in 1792.[77]

The right of life and death, though analogous to the full
*potestas* of the Roman house-father, never reached this complete development with the Virginia master.   The law intervened to give the slave first, a limited protection against his

<hr/>

[77] Hening, II., 299, 481, 482; III., 459; IV., 169; VIII., 136, 358;
*Statutes at Large,* n. s., I., 125 ; *Revised Code,* 1819, II., 285.

master, and finally as full protection as any other person, bond or free. Until 1723, if a slave chanced to die under or in consequence of lawful correction it was viewed as merely a lamentable and "accidental homicide." An act of that year declared such killing of a slave to be manslaughter only, and not liable to prosecution or punishment. But if a single credible witness affirmed before the county court that the slave was killed "wilfully, maliciously, or designedly," the perpetrator might be indicted, and, if convicted, punished as a murderer On account of a case of revolting cruelty in the murder of his slave by one John Huston, which came up at the December term of the General Court in 1788, in which the offender was convicted only of manslaughter by the jury, and so went scot free, the General Assembly, then in session, was induced by members of the court to repeal the law of 1723, so that thenceforth the killing and maiming of a slave were punishable as if he were a free white man. There was nothing, however, to prevent excessive beating of a slave that did not result in death or maiming, except the "deep and solemn reprobation of the tribunal of public opinion," though a person who cruelly beat a horse or other beast was subject to a fine of $50.[18]

In 1850 another case of cruelty toward a slave occurred that had an important effect upon the law. The case involving beating to death with torture, was first passed upon by the Circuit Court of Hanover, which sentenced the master to five years in the penitentiary. This penalty was so manifestly inadequate to the offense that the case was carried up to the General Court, where it was unanimously adjudged not manslaughter, but murder in the first degree, the presiding judge declaring as his belief, "The records of criminal jurisprudence do not contain a case of more atrocious and wicked cruelty." In this, however, he was mistaken. A case similar and more

---

[18] Hening, IV., 133; XII., 681; Minor, *Institutes*, I., 185; Randolph, *Reports*, V., 686; *Statutes*, 1847–48, p. 112; 1849, 740.

6

brutal had occurred in English possessions as far back as 1811. Arthur Hodge, Esq., a gentleman by birth, was tried by jury, condemned and hung in Tortola, one of the Virgin islands, for the murder of several slaves by whipping them without intermission for over an hour, one of whom was lashed to a tree when he could no longer stand, and whipped till he fainted, and another till his black skin could not be seen. They were then carried to the " sick house " and allowed to die without medical attention. He had tortured other slaves by pouring boiling water down their throats, eventually causing their death, or by dipping them in kettles of boiling liquid and burning them in the mouth with hot irons, and by inflicting successive " cart-whippings " at " short-quarters,"[79] or loading them with heavy irons or chains. This man was the owner of some one hundred and thirty slaves, most of whom had experienced his cruelty. This special example in Virginia, however, was of extreme barbarity, and was so notorious that homicide of a slave by excessive whipping was hereafter viewed as murder in the first degree without regard to the offender's intent.[80]

The slave was a legal person as regarded his criminal acts, and had the same liability as other free agents. There was, however, a discrimination against the slave to his disadvantage in methods of punishment and procedure, designed to act as a preventive influence upon others of his class. Prior to 1692 slaves guilty of capital crimes were entitled to the same procedure, including jury trial, as free whites. But the charges, delay, and uncertainty incident to this method of the General Court, obstructed prosecution and encouraged such a dangerous increase of crime that it was found necessary to institute a special tribunal at this time for the express and

---

[79] Belisario and Hetherington, *Report of the Trial of Arthur Hodge, Esquire*, 8-20, 135, 170–186. In this punishment the whip was shortened so as to go around the whole body, striking the front as well as the back.

[80] Grattan, *Reports*, VII., 673, 681.

"speedy prosecution" of slaves. The criminal was to be arrested and safely imprisoned in the county jail, and the governor upon notification of the committment by the sheriff issued a commission of *oyer* and *terminer* to fit persons of the county, who immediately arraigned and indicted the offender publicly at the court-house. "Confession of the party, or the oaths of two witnesses, or of one with pregnant circumstances," was sufficient evidence to convict, and judgment was passed without the intervention of jury, and execution awarded. When this law was revised in 1705 the master was allowed to appear in defense of his slave as to matters of fact but not as to technicalities of procedure, and he was indemnified for the value of the slave condemned. In 1723 the evidence of negroes, mulattoes, or Indians, bond or free, sustained by pregnant circumstances, or the testimony of "one or more credible witnesses," was sufficient to acquit or convict. To deter non-Christian colored persons from bearing false witness they were threatened, before giving evidence, with the pillory, loss of both ears, and thirty-nine lashes upon "his or her bare back for false testimony." By the revisal of 1748, ten days respite was given between sentence and execution, and unanimity of the court was made necessary for conviction. If there was a difference of opinion the result was acquittal. In practice the commissions were generally issued to justices of the peace, but as a separate one was required in each case, and this was expensive and troublesome, and sometimes involved the difficulty of the commission's determining before the judgment could be carried into execution, a law of 1765 vested the power to try slaves in the justices of the county courts by a general commission of *oyer* and *terminer* issued with that constituting a justice. Any four or more of the justices, one being a quorum, constituted the court and had jurisdiction as before.

In the latter half of the eighteenth century the rigor of the criminal code was greatly diminished. The power of dismemberment vested in the county court, where outlying slaves could not be corrected by other means, had been exercised by inflicting castration, first upon slaves threatening rape and then as a punishment common to this class, whence danger was thought to come.  This extension, however, was resented by public sentiment, as "disproportionate to the offense and contrary to the principles of humanity," and the ability of the county court to order castration was limited to cases of blacks convicted of an "attempt to ravish a white woman." [81]   One of the Revolutionary bills of 1779, enacted in 1786, extended the period between sentence and execution, fixing the minimum at thirty days as in the case of white men, except in conspiracy, insurrection, and rebellion.  The court had now to consist of at least five justices, and no one who had an interest in the slave could be a member of it.  Unanimity was still necessary for conviction and only undoubted slaves were tried without jury.  Any slave suing for his freedom was prosecuted and tried as a free man.  In 1790, the hustings court of Richmond, composed of the mayor, recorder, and aldermen, or any five of them, was given a jurisdiction like that of the county courts over slaves, but Williamsburg and Norfolk were denied this right.  In 1797, however, magistrates of the corporation courts were given a criminal jurisdiction as to slaves.  Before 1792 no exception could be taken to the trial, but thereafter it could, and the justices were obliged also to allow counsel at the master's expense.  The tendency towards mitigating the legal position of the slave was further shown by expunging from the code at this time everything relative to the outlawry of slaves.[82]

In the case of free men criminal procedure was very different.  They were allowed examination before the court of the county in which the offense was committed, and acquittal by

---

[81] Hening, III., 102, 103, 270; IV., 127, 128; VI., 105; VIII., 137, 138, 858; *Dinwiddie Papers*, I., 384.  Governor Dinwiddie says the indemnity was "an encouragement to people to discover the villainies of their slaves."

[82] Hening, XII., 345; XIII., 200; *Statutes at Large*, n. s., II., 78.

it was final. If convicted by it, the concurrent action first of a grand jury with the agreement of twelve jurors, and then of a petit jury of the county by unanimous verdict, was necessary to pronounce one guilty. A motion in arrest of judgment was open to him by which he might take exception to the proceedings, and unanimity between his judges as between his jurors was necessary to condemnation. In some cases, also, in punishment free men secured the benefit of clergy denied to slaves for the same offense. But as to trial the main difference now left was that slaves were not allowed the intervention of a jury. As Judge St. George Tucker has well shown this was not a disadvantage, but a benefit. A court of five justices was more select than an ordinary jury of the county, and far more likely to do justice to the slave. Their opinions were given "openly, immediately, and seriatim," commencing with the youngest judge, and if a single one favored the slave he was acquitted. But in jury trial votes were secret, and a few objectors might be won over for conviction by the desire to be relieved of enforced confinement. Unanimity of the jury was not only necessary for conviction but for acquittal, so that a slave's chances of escape with a jury as ordinarily constituted were regarded as very small.[83]

As to punishment, offenses fell into two distinct classes— (1) those punishable with loss of life or limb, chiefly capital crimes, and (2) those punishable by whipping in lieu of fine and imprisonment, which was imposed upon free whites; or by pillory or mutilation, common in certain cases to whites and blacks. The capital crimes by the code of 1748 were: to plot (1) rebellion, (2) insurrection, or (3) murder; (4) to prepare, exhibit or administer, without the order or consent of superiors, medicines with intent to poison; (5) manslaughter, (6) house-breaking at night, (7) burglary of 20 s. value, (8) third offense of hog-stealing by white or black. These were

---

[83] Tucker, *Blackstone,* appendix., 55–63.

declared felony without the benefit of clergy, and were punished by death. A crime punishable by dismemberment was (9) attempted rape. Capital crimes within clergy were: (1) administering medicine without bad intent or consequence, as this had now become a practice dangerous both to whites and blacks with the rise of the negro "doctor;" (2) manslaughter of slave, in 1764; (3) house-breaking, not burglary, in 1772; and (4) by 1796 all cases which applied to whites except rebellion, insurrection, murder, or administering medicine with bad intent. Benefit of clergy was here construed to substitute for death burning in the hand, and, for colored persons, whipping also within the discretion of the court. Upon a second conviction for these offenses the benefit of clergy was denied and the death penalty inflicted. In 1775, transportation "to any of the foreign West Indies" was substituted, where feasible, as a humane commutation for the death penalty of slaves in arms against the colony or in the possession of the enemy. By an act of 1801 the governor and council were empowered to sell slaves under sentence of death for transportation out of the United States, the transportation acting as a reprieve, except that if the criminal returned he was to be executed. The courts also could by unanimous, but not by majority, verdict order transportation in lieu of conviction of felony. By a law of 1847, this commutation for the death penalty by sale and transportation beyond the limits of United States could be extended at the discretion of the court to all crimes except those for which a free white person would suffer death. In 1857 the governor was allowed to employ such slaves, in lieu of immediate sale and transportation, upon the public works, as negro convicts were employed. By a law of 1805 several additions were made to capital crimes raising their number to ten. To wilfully and maliciously "set fire to a barn, stable, corn-house, or other outhouse, or to be accessory to a black so doing, and to attempt to ravish a white woman were made felonies punishable by death. To burn a stack of grain or hay, however, was within benefit of clergy and punished by burning in the hand and 39 lashes.[84]

The chief discrimination against the slave involved in punishment for capital crimes was that bare intention or attempt to commit a felony, though unsuccessful or not resulting in actual breach of the peace, was punishable as if the offense had been committed, while in the case of free whites intention was not punishable as it was in the case of slaves, unless the deed were committed  An attempt against the virtue of a white woman by a free white was a high misdemeanor, not a capital crime.  Free negroes were likewise punished by confinement in the penitentiary for three or more years for many crimes that were capital in the slave.

Crimes of the second class in the nature of misdemeanors were: (1) hog stealing, first offense; (2) unseasonable killing of deer, if on the slave's own responsibility; (3) presence at unlawful meetings; (4) going abroad without leave; (5) carrying offensive or defensive weapons or ammunition without permission; (6) raising his hand against a Christian white unless wantonly assaulted.  The penalty in each case was corporal punishment upon the bare back, the number of lashes, varying from ten to thirty-nine, being specifically stated.  Free colored persons and whites received like punishment, though a fewer number of lashes, where like the slave they could not make satisfaction by money payment.  By 1847 the crimes of (7) provoking language, as well as a menacing gesture to a white; (8) making a seditious speech; and (9) selling, keeping or administering medicine in other families without consent, were specifically added, and punishment was not to exceed thirty-nine lashes at one time.  A money commutation to be paid by any one for the slave was suggested by the revisors of this law, but the provision was finally stricken out.  Crimes somewhat more aggravated, and

---

[84] Hening, VI., 104–112, 122; IX., 106; *Statutes at Large*, n. s., II., 279; III., 119; Grattan, *Reports*, XV., 561; Code, 1849, p. 753; Code, 1860, 121.

punishable by pillory and loss of ears in addition to whipping, were: (1) the second offense of hog stealing, and (2) false witness. A number of offenses, however, from their nature imputed only to free persons in their relations with slaves or others, and punishable with fine, imprisonment, stripes and death, the slave as an innocent or aggrieved person escaped. For instance, a slave went unpunished for marriage with a white; nor was he capable of forgery or treason or kidnapping and selling a free person as a slave. The act of 1865–66, which abolished slavery and servitude, except for crime, repealed all the laws concerning slaves and made the criminal laws applicable to whites apply equally to colored persons, except where "otherwise specially provided." [85]

The discrimination against the negro and Indian, slave or free, has the appearance of greater rigor than actually was the case. The severity of the punishment was designed as a deterrent influence, say the statutes, and judging from results it was remarkably successful. Speedy trial and execution accomplished legally what is now unsuccessfully attempted through the methods of 'lynch law.' Dismemberment and death were penalties in no sense comparable with the crime of rape, yet the rarity of that offense during the slave *régime* is an eloquent commentary on the success of the principle of absolute subjection as applied to the half savage African and Indian. During the troublous times of the first three years of the war when, if ever, the slaves would seize their opportunity, the few that were condemned, executed or reprieved for transportation is shown by the appropriation of only $25,000 for their value. [86]

The harsher discriminations of the law were practically abolished before the close of the eighteenth century, and, in the opinion of the two most distinguished anti-slavery leaders

---

[85] Tucker, *Slavery*, 64, 65, 66; Statutes, 1822–23. p. 37; Hening, III., 179, 180, 277, 662; IV., 108, 129, 266; VI., 108, 122; Statutes, 1847–48, 135, 126; Code, 1849, 754, note; Revised Code, 1819, II., 16.
[86] Session Acts, 1863, p. 85.

in Virginia, Thomas Jefferson and St. George Tucker, the previous provisions were the result, not of inhumanity, but of "those political considerations indispensably necessary where slavery prevails to any great extent." They felt, too, that the treatment of American slaves was "milder than in any other country" where there were so many slaves or so large a proportion as compared with free persons. Law and customary treatment together served to a remarkable degree the purpose of preventing that large growth of individual crime that has come with this class of population in its free condition, relieved of the extraordinary restraints of slavery and of discrimination. The rarity of the appearance of the slave in the annals of the higher crimes in comparison with the whites and free negroes is conspicuous. His commonest offenses were petty crimes or those arising from the collusion or influence of others, such as, absconding or insurrection, in which whites and free negroes often played the chief part.[87]

Insurrection was more of an anticipated danger than an actual one. As soon as negro population became at all formidable, energetic measures were taken to prevent the possibility of revolt, and they were largely successful. Though a number of attempted or supposed conspiracies were discovered during the seventeenth and eighteenth centuries, no actual insurrection worthy of the name occurred until the nineteenth, when the rigor of slavery and slave legislation was past. Absconding and outlying servants and slaves or assemblies, incited and aided by Indians, whites—especially convicts and foreigners—and free negroes were a convenient nucleus for combined action, and for this reason restrictive and punitive legislation was especially directed toward them. In this connection was developed a system of police patrol known and feared among the negroes as the "Paterollers."[88]

---

[87] Tucker, *Slavery*, 67; Jefferson, *Notes*, 259.
[88] This patrol has been memorialized in the negro plantation melody,
"Run nigger, run, de pateroller'll ketch you;
Run nigger, run, till ye allmos daid," etc.

Slaves were freely allowed to go anywhere with their masters' written consent, and were permitted and required to assemble at church on Sundays or other days for worship; but their other assemblies at feasts and burials, and during the holidays which they enjoyed at Christmas, Easter, and Whitsuntide, when left to themselves, became turbulent and had to be restricted by law. The militia was kept in as efficient and well disciplined a condition as the law could make it to be a threat against any outbreak, nor was it withdrawn in force from any part of the colony in the early days. Arms and ammunition were denied the dangerous classes, white and black, except on the frontiers, where they were essential to protection.

Between 1680 and 1726 there were a number of scares from negro assemblies or plots, and in the latter year the Assembly established an occasional patrol by directing portions of the county militia under the order of the county lieutenant, whenever need arose, to disperse unusual concourses of negroes or slaves and to see to the apprehension of criminals. In 1738 the chief officer of the county militia was empowered to appoint, toward June of each year, a yearly patrol, its members to be paid for their service by exemption from taxes. This consisted of an officer and four militiamen, who at proper times visited all negro quarters as well as " other places suspected of entertaining unlawful assemblies of slaves, servants, or disorderly persons." They had the power to arrest all such persons or strolling slaves and servants without passes, and to take them to a justice to be whipped not exceeding twenty lashes. In later days a justice of the county court appointed the chief officer and as many men as were needed for a patrol. They made a written report to the court every three months and were paid, the captain one dollar, and the men seventy-five cents, for every twelve hours' service. The patrol was now required to make its round at least once a month. In towns the corporation courts divided the city into wards and appointed one or more captains in each, requiring the patrol to be on duty at least once a week. Another function of the patrol was to search for firearms, and when acting on a warrant it could break open and enter the houses of free negroes and of slaves in the absence of their masters. A special patrol, a captain and three men, was provided for by an act of 1855–56, whenever five slave-holders petitioned the county court for it, to recapture fugitive slaves. It was paid a reasonable compensation from the fugitive slave tax and the master also was assessed, according to distance, from $40 to $100 for the captive.[89] When the slaves escaped to a great distance special methods and rewards had to be provided for their recovery, and these in the absence of a national fugitive slave law were not often successful. A reward of 15 per cent. of the value of the slave was offered for those returned from Allegheny, Washington, and Frederick counties, Maryland, and 25 per cent. of his value if returned from a free State. For the nearer counties on the Ohio and Potomac 10 per cent. only was offered. For slaves captured in Ohio, Pennsylvania or Indiana a reward of 50 per cent. and mileage 20 cents a mile, and if in New England, New York or Canada $120. It is not surprising that the fugitive slave law passed by Congress in 1850 was strongly urged by the Virginia legislature.

The rebellions or insurrections of slaves were all local, yet their influence upon general slave legislation was not confined to Virginia, but showed itself in the restrictive laws of a number of slave States. The incorporation of slaves into the acts against runaways, the provisions against outlying slaves, the

---

[89] Hening, III., 87, 536; IV., 126, 202; V., 19; Revised Code, 1819, II., 288; Statutes, 1831–32, 19, 20; 1839, 24; 1849, 445; 1855, 38; 1860, 795. *Virginia MSS.*, B. R. O., 1694, Nov. 5, p. 206; *Ibid.*, Vol. II., pt. 2, p. 579; *Ibid.*, Gooch to Lords of Trade, 17–4, June 29; Drysdale to Lords of Trade, 1722, December 20; *Dinwiddie Papers*, II., 345, 474; *Byrd, MSS.*, II., 240. Gov. Gooch criticises Sir Wm. Keith for advocating in his history the use of arms by slaves and servants, saying, "by the use of arms he exposes their throats to be cut by their slaves or by a worse and more dangerous enemy, the shoals of convicts." These were only controlled by the terror of a militia. Gov. Drysdale said to the Lords of Trade in 1722 that severe laws were the only means of preventing insurrections.

chief restrictions of the codes of 1705 and 1748 and of the law of 1723 were either directly or indirectly connected with the prevention of this offense. Any number of negroes or slaves over five conspiring for murder or rebellion were declared by the law of 1723 felons punishable with death. A plot by a less number was not considered to be a conspiracy worthy of the name insurrection. Of such conspiracies which might, but for fortuitous circumstances, have become insurrections on a large scale, only two occurred in the history of Virginia. One of these, known as Gabriel's Attempt, was directed against the city of Richmond in 1800, with the design of seizing the city at night, killing the males, dividing the females, and then arming for the extermination of the whites throughout the State. It was planned by two young and intelligent negroes; Gabriel, a slave, twenty-four years old, and one Jack Bowler, aged twenty-eight, neither of whom had an especial personal grievance to inspire him. They organized as many as 1,000 negroes in Henrico county, arming them with scythes and knives, and marched toward the city during the night. Forced to halt by a stream swollen and impassible from a recent storm, they disbanded, expecting to renew the attempt on the following night. But fortunately their plot was disclosed by a slave Pharaoh, who had escaped from them and aroused the citizens of Richmond before the attack could be made. A reward of $300 was offered for the leaders, Gabriel and Jack. They were caught and executed, but a large number of the conspirators were mercifully acquitted or the charges against them were dismissed on account of lack of evidence. This plot resulted in the institution of a public guard for the city, of 68 persons under a captain and other officers.[90]

[90] Hening, II., 275, 481, 493; III., 86, 459; IV., 126, 128; V., 108; XII., 182; Journal House of Delegates, 1849-50, p. 240; United States Statutes, IX., 462, c. 60; *Dinwiddie Papers,* Vol. II., 102, 103; Howison, *Virginia,* II., 390; *Richmond Examiner,* September 17 and 30, 1800; *Virginian,* January 1, 1808; Statutes at Large, II., 295, 296; Order Book, Henrico County Court, No. 9.

A smaller but more successful attempt than this was that of Nat Turner, a well-educated and well-treated negro preacher of Southampton County, in 1831. He was looked upon from early childhood as a prophet by his kindred, and by flattery, omens and misconception of passages of Scripture was brought to a fanatical state of mind in which he supposed he was called upon to deliver his race from bondage. His chief adherents and organizers were Hark and Will, fellow slaves, and Artis, a free negro. Starting with some four or five persons, armed with only a hatchet and an axe, the band rapidly grew by impressment as the raiders advanced, or as runaways joined it, to twenty negroes, and, finally, to forty. They seized horses and arms at the various places visited, and from Sunday night, to noon of the following day they terrorized without serious opposition the whole country side. The most cruel murders, of men, women, and children were committed in their rapid house-to-house advance toward the county-seat, but strange to say only a single well authenticated case of attempted violation of a female occurred. Some sixty persons were killed. People were taken utterly by surprise; their houses were open as usual in the hot summer nights, and most of the males in the county were absent at a religious meeting in North Carolina. But as the alarm spread the whites quickly raised a sufficient force to check the advance and prevent the escape of the negroes to the Dismal Swamp. Most of the raiders, including Nat, were finally captured.[91] A most impartial trial was given to all, except a few decapitated at Cross Keys, admitting not only negro and slave testimony, as usual in criminal trials of slaves, but even the testimony of members of the band in their own behalf. Many escaped punishment by help of their masters or because they had been forced to join the raiders. Twenty-one were convicted and condemned,

---

[91] *Richmond Enquirer*, August 30, 1831; *Richmond Whig*, September 26, August 29, 1831; *Norfolk Herald*, 1831; Howison, *Virginia*, II., 439.

but only thirteen were executed.    None, not even Nat, testified that cruel treatment had been a cause of the insurrection.[92] [¶]The consequences alarmed not only the other counties of the Black Belt, but the whole State, and neighboring slave States, even to Louisiana.    It was thought in the excited state of public feeling that it was only a part of a wide-spread slave revolt, but it was purely local.    Governor Floyd, thinking that influence had come from other States, urged a revision of slave laws and the expulsion of the free blacks.    The slave trade was restricted by several Southern States and a number of farmers emigrated.    In a desire to get rid of negroes the questions of emancipation and colonization were brought up

---

[92] Fanaticism followed the mental aberration of Nat which was brought to a climax by an eclipse and the consequent peculiar appearance of the sun, and he "conjured," as the negroes say, his followers by means that readily appealed to their ignorance and superstition, such as; "hieroglyphics," "numbers," and "signs written in blood."

The effect of even ordinary solar phenomena upon negro intelligence is well illustrated by the following occurrence, quoted from the *Baltimore Sun*, May 13, 1899: "Richmond, May 12.    A rare sight was presented here to-day.    For several hours concentric rainbows of great brilliancy surrounded the sun.    Between the luminous circles rested dense clouds, and all was bright without the outer circle.    It inspired admiration in the eyes of intelligent people, but the ignorant were deeply affected with fear.    For hours the people stood in the streets watching the beautiful phenomena with the naked eye and smoked glass.    Many colored people experienced great fear, and the Rev. John Jasper [a noted negro divine], whose opinions on planetary movements stand higher with them than any other authority, was asked by members of his flock to interpret the sign in the heavens. The old philosopher, now eighty-seven years old, is nearly blind with age. He listened attentively to the description of the solar halo, and after a few seconds of deep meditation, said: 'It is a sign God has placed in the sky to warn the people of his wrath to come.    Wickedness is increasing, and the way most people are carrying on is simply scandalous.    The Bible says strange sights shall appear in the sky, and I believe this is one of them.' His flock breathed easier when the sun reached the meridian and the phenomena disappeared."

For a complete and interesting account from fuller sources of the Southampton or Nat Turner insurrection see Dr. W. S. Drewry's *The Southampton Insurrection*.

in the next legislature of Virginia, but were decided adversely, and stringent legislation was enacted against meetings and education of slaves, particularly of preachers, and against inciting revolts. To advocate rebellion by means of writing or printing was made a penitentiary offense, and to express the opinions that masters had no right to their slaves was punished by a fine of $500 and one year in jail. To advise conspiracy was treason against the State and the penalty was death. Another direct result of this revolt was the revisal of the provision of the act of 1830–31, that no white be allowed to assemble slaves to instruct them in reading and writing, by the addition of amendments against the preaching of slaves or of free negroes, and forbidding them to attend religious meetings at night without permission.

So in these last days of slavery was added another legal incident to their condition, *i. e.;* (19) *non-instruction* in the elements of *secular* education. The right to (20) *religious instruction* was not, however, seriously restricted by either law or custom. An act of 1804 defining unlawful meetings of slaves had included night-meetings at places of worship as dangerous on account of plots, but as the effect of this was thought to infringe the " religious rights " of slaves in excluding them from night preaching, often customary, an act was passed at the next session, January 4, 1805, allowing slaves to go with any member of the family of their owners to any religious service conducted by an ordained white minister or by a layman. A master also was allowed to employ any free person to give religious instruction to his slaves or he gave them written consent to go elsewhere for it. Prior to 1804, meetings at church on Sunday or any other day to attend service had been specifically exempted from the list of unlawful meetings. Another legal right of the slave was (21) *support and protection.* In general, custom was a sufficient guaranty of this right, but the law intervened to establish fully the master's obligation and to prevent its being shifted upon the State in the case of old, infirm, and disabled slaves.

Medical attention and nursing for the sick were recognized duties, and if old and infirm slaves were given away, sold or freed to escape their charge the county justices could proceed against either the seller or the donee for the support of the slaves.[93]

The legal condition of the slave resulting then from this legislation finds its analogue not so much in ancient slavery or in European serfdom, both of which were harsher in their incidents, as in the institution of mediaeval villainage, particularly that of England, which as regards services, punishment, property, and personal incidents applying to an upper class of non-free men was strikingly like slavery as developed in Virginia and some other American States.

*Social Status of the Slave.*—Customary institutional development, in general, precedes and is a source of legal, but as on the one hand law may originate new incidents, so many customary practices may continue without the sanction of law or even in direct contravention of legal provisions. Frequently such practices as are sanctioned at the bar of public opinion tend to exert a mitigating influence upon the condition of dependents, but in cases they may and have assumed a harsher character than is consistent with principles of law and humanity, and require the restraining influence of the courts or of the legislature. As regards slavery, a customary status thus arose from the practical exercise by the ruling class of powers, authorized but not enjoined by law, and from customs in accord or even contrary to the spirit of the law, a status that was distinctly marked from the strict legal one defined by positive legislation.

The separation between these two conditions of the slave was analogous to, but not so extensive as, that developed also

---

[93] Statutes at Large, n. s., 1804, p. 108; 1805, p. 124; Hening, IV., 129; Virginia Code, 1860, p. 510.

in the practical treatment of white servants,[94] for two important reasons. The first was the inferior race and religion of
the negro, mulatto, and Indian servant or slave which separated this class socially by a more impassable barrier from the
mass even of the whites than mere legal status would have
done. The second was, that slaves were not to any extent at
first recognized as a source of eventual or possible free men,
who with their new status and citizenship might demand
social as well as legal equality. When this probability arose,
considerations of race purity and inferior civilization were
strong enough to refer the free colored person to a social status
practically identical with that of the slave and to a legal status
similar in many of its disabilities to slavery.[95] Its tendency,
too, was to define more strictly caste distinctions and to
increase the social and legal disabilities of the slave.

In custom the conception of the personality of the slave
tended to supplant that of property, and was recognized to a
far greater extent than accorded with the strict letter of the
law. The slave was here viewed as a human being possessed
of like emotions, desires, and ambitions as free men and whites,
many of which might be reasonably gratified without impair-
ing any obligation of service due the master. Even practices
in which damage was a possible or even certain result to the
property element found a continuing sanction in custom. The
common recognition of marital and family rights, for instance,
was the outgrowth of a sentiment of humanity rather than of
economic interest. That the ties so established were always
accorded the full recognition they deserved is by no means
true, but their existence, even when hampered, distinctly
mitigated the conditions of slavery.[96] So also slave-breeding,

---

[94] Cf. Ballagh, *White Servitude*, 68 *et seq.*
[95] Chastellux, *Travels*, II., 190, 200; Revised Code, Supplement, 234,
244, 246, 247; Leigh, *Reports*, IV., 652.
[96] Call, *Reports*, II., 17, Fitzhugh *et ux. vs.* Foote; Hening, III., 334;
IV., 21; Smith, *Philosophy and Practice of Slavery*, 314.

7

however unfortunate some of its applications may have been, had its origin in humanity. Its development prevented the introduction of the barbarous practice of the Spanish West Indies, where marriage was denied because it was cheaper to import slaves than to raise them. The abuse of breeding in the prostitution of female slaves was not only lessened by heavy legal and social penalties, but met a natural check in the density of population, whose increase even the domestic slave trade, a necessity for the existence of slavery in the old States, was unable to prevent. The desire to procreate slaves when they were cheap was anything but economic in cause or effect. The damage to service in childbearing and the cost of rearing the infant was viewed as involving a net loss, and as one of the burdens incident to a human slave system. It was upon this economic ground that conscientious anti-slavery slave-holders were wont to base their strongest arguments. Slave-breeding in the opprobrious use of the term probably had an extensive existence with a certain class, which was governed neither by economic nor moral considerations, but as this class is usually small in any civilized society and as historic evidence shows its limited extent in Virginia, the offense was kept within bounds by public sentiment and legal penalties.

The disposition on the part of the upper classes to recognize their wardship [97] of the dependent is very marked, but duty was not the only tie that bound the master to his slave. Mutual affection often characterised the relation. The property element in the slave was not until the later days of the institution regarded as a speculative value. A master generally sold his slaves only when they were unruly or worthless or when he was too poor to keep them. Like that of land and stock, the accumulation of slaves tended constantly to exceed the limit of true economy. They were the badge of social distinction, and rank followed acres and servants more closely than

[97] Smith, *Philosophy and Practice of Slavery*, 278–328.

financial solvency. A gentleman might often be a bankrupt, but he must have slaves, and the last thing he parted with to discharge his obligations of honor were his mahogany, his dependents, and his habits. Many families in the agricultural depression of the last decades of the first half of the nineteenth century were bankrupt by their slaves, whom they could not in the slave's interest, or would not for their own convenience, turn into cash from the slave dealer. This feeling was fully reciprocated by the slave. "There are hundreds of slaves," said a distinguished professor of William and Mary College, " who will desert parents, wives or husbands, brothers and sisters to follow a kind master." [98]

The tie of master and servant (slave) was looked upon as second only to that of husband and wife, parent and child, brother and sister. In the Southampton insurrection many armed their slaves for their defense, and in several instances the whites, especially women, escaped only through the help of slaves. Notably at one place the slaves resolutely opposed Nat Turner's gang, declaring they would " lose every drop of blood in defense of their master and his family." Even at this time the slaves were felt to be generally well affected and faithful to their masters, and the nobility of those who risked their lives for their white masters received appropriate public recognition. In view of the sectional feeling displayed in the heated debate on the Foot Resolution, Senator Smith, of Virginia, said that in an emergency he would rely solely upon his own slaves for his defense. The testimony of those who took part in the famous debate in the Virginia assembly in 1831–32 on the emancipation of slaves, when the anti-slavery leaders put forward their strongest arguments against the institution, bears witness to this mutual attachment, and to the kind treatment and abundant support given the slave. Many a slave passed through life without ever having had a blow from master or overseer; and in the western parts of

[98] Dew, *Debate of* 1831–32.

Virginia, a grazing country where slaves were not so numerous as in the eastern counties, they were treated, and acted, more like day laborers than slaves, enjoying as many comforts and as much spare time as fell to the lot of the poor whites.[99]

The institution in many respects was then patriarchal. The slave was a member of the family, often a privileged member. His master's goods and honor and prosperity were his own. He could not steal from his master, but only appropriated articles legitimately to his use as necessity arose. This habit, unchecked by indulgent masters, in some degree explains the moral obliquity of the ordinary negro in petty theft. The master was the supporter, director, defender of his dependents, but in sickness, death and disaster the faithful slave was often the actual legatee of the cares and responsibilities of the estate and the virtual guardian of his owner's property and children. He was playmate, pedagogue, brother, exemplar, friend and companion of the white from the cradle to the grave. His family pride far surpassed that of his owners. It was he that set apart and scorned the poor whites as " po' white trash," who were a lower order of society in his opinion, fit to associate only with other social pariahs, and not with " quality folks " like himself and his master. It was he, too, that detested the " free negro," as neither a member of the family nor of industrial society, but an improvident and grumbling idler, living by theft or charity. As the hoary-headed patriarch who had seen several generations of the family born and buried he was the embodiment of wisdom and tyranny. His sway was despotic over all his juniors, young and old, white and black. He was the relative of the family, titled by merit not by grace, " Uncle " and " Mammy." He was hugged and kissed by the children, honored and respected by

[99] *Richmond Enquirer*, August 30, 1831; *Examiner*, September 19 and 30, 1900; *Whig*, September 26, August 25, 29, 1831; *Norfolk Herald*, August, 1831; *Madison Pamphlets*, Vol. 14, 110–133; Minor, *Institutes*, I., 185; Randolph, *Reports*, V., 586; Olmstead, *Slave States*, 154.

their elders. His opinion was consulted and generally followed in his own domain. He had the freedom of the home
and of the plantation. He was an indispensable factor at
grand social functions. His own anniversaries were celebrated,
and his death was mourned as a personal and not as a property loss.[100]

Such were a few among the noblest fruits of domestic
slavery. But there were both light and shade. There was no
appropriate reward of merit which the tried and trusted slave
might not aspire to and actually receive, but the slothful, the
inexperienced, the disorderly and corrupt were dealt with to
the full extent of the law. The reward of virtue was of
grace, sanctioned and commanded by custom and to a limited
extent by law. The reward of vice was a certainty. It met
its penalty in law, and, in cases, more grievous penalty in
custom. The choice lay not with the inferior, but with the
superior. It was partly this that led Jefferson and Tucker,
looking forward from the institution they knew in the eighteenth century, to predict[101] the debauchery of public and
private morals, the prostitution of youth, and the bestializa-
tion of both master and slave. To Jefferson, too, it supported
an unrepublican form of government, perpetuating and enhanc-
ing a caste system that was inconsistent with a realization of
the true ideal of democratic equality upon which the new
state and nation should be constituted. But to Dabney, Dew,
and the later generations of apologists, looking backward
upon actual rather than possible effects, both in politics and
society, it produced a chivalrous, honorable, princely and
hospitable aristocracy best fitted to rule a state and nation;
while it conquered, civilized and christianized a savage.[102]

---

[100] Dabney, *Defense of Virginia*, 319, 321; Fitzhugh, *Cannibals All*, 296, 301,
302; Fitzhugh, *Sociology*, 245–248, 279; Olmstead, *Slave States*, 46.

[101] *Letters from Virginia*, 73–103; Jefferson, *Notes*; Tucker, *Blackstone*;
Appendix.

[102] Fitzhugh, *Sociology*, 84, *et seq.*; Dabney, 215, *et seq.*; Smith, *Philosophy
and Practice of Slavery*, 176–192, 228–257.

To the one the good effects were an accident, to the other the evil. Both were partly right and partly wrong. Humanity and virtue were as characteristic of the administration of masters as cruelty and recklessness were of the far-away overseer or domestic slave-trader. But with the institution as a whole, bad treatment was the exception rather than the rule. The barbarity of chaining together, to prevent escape, members of a band of melancholy captives bound to the lands of the Ohio or the Mississippi, was more apparent than real. But the separation of husband and wife, parent and child, never in life to meet or hear of the other again, as was not an infrequent result in the dispersion of the estates of descedents and bankrupts, though sanctioned by law, was from a white man's point of view a curse little short of a crime. So, also, the lash of the pitiless overseer or slave-driver, the passion of the unscrupulous owner or superior might inflict pain and indignity without any adequate check in law or custom where the good will of the patron was lacking to his defenseless dependent.

The maintenance of the slave in contrast with that of the servant was an obligation left almost wholly to the regulation of custom. Motives of humanity and interest were considered sufficient impulses to control the master's action here without the intervention of legislation,[103] and the scarcity of complaints as compared with those of servants shows that the assumption was fully justified. This duty included food, clothing, housing and medical atttention. Food was simple, nourishing and abundant. It consisted chiefly of fat and salt meat, field peas, beans, pumpkins, melons and common vegetables, corn bread in its various forms of the "pone," "hoe-cake," "ash-cake," "dodgers," and "scratch-backs," and a kind of molasses called "black-strap," "pot-licker," and sometimes "possum" and persimmon-beer; apple-butter,

---

[103] Olmstead, *Slave States*, 37, 44, 110–112; Dabney, *Defense of Virginia*, 273, 274; Virginia Code, 1849, Cap. 10; Hundley, *Social Relations*, 84 *et seq.*

and often cider or milk were common in the back country. A kind of food suited to their taste and that would make able-bodied workmen was sought, and it was practically the same as that at present in general use among negro and white laborers in the various southern States. Clothing was plain and coarse, home-made by the mistress, the housekeeper, the domestics and cobblers on the plantation, or imported from England and the North. Two all-around outfits were given to each slave during the year at times best suited to his comfort and pleasure. The tax upon the energies of the female members of the family among the middle-class planters, who spent their evenings and the long winter days in providing the clothing, was a serious obstruction to the pleasure and mental improvement they might otherwise have enjoyed.[104] It has been said with much truth that the master and mistress were the greatest slaves on the plantation. The negro cabins were comfortable one or two-room houses for separate families, built of logs, the cracks between them being stopped with wood and plaster. They were the "log and daubed" houses still common and were much superior to the frontiersman's cabin. But often, also, they were built of substantial brick with a second story, inner fittings and windows of glass, far more commodious and comfortable than the average laboring free man of the South, white or black, is able to erect for himself. Sometimes, especially on the smaller plantations, they were scattered on either side in the rear of but near the manor house, and might be connected with it or with the kitchens by covered ways. More often on the large estates such provision was made only for the domestics, while cabins of the field workers were grouped in some shady grove at a greater distance from the house and were known as "quarters."[105] These might be in charge of a negro or white overseer, who was

[104] Dabney, *Virginia,* 276 ; Hundley, *Social Relations in our Southern States,* 84–90.

[105] Olmstead, *Slave States,* 27, 28, 44, 110, 111, 112.

responsible for peace and order, but any damage done by the slaves where there was no white overseer was assessed upon the master.[106]      When masters owned a number of plantations or farms in different parts of the State, all except the domain were usually under the control of overseers who lived in quarters with the "gang" of laborers, servants and slaves.

In absenteeism the personal bond between master and slave was undoubtedly weakened and the economic bond of identical interest between capital and labor, though it might be strong, was but a poor substitute for mutual affection. Much depended upon the personality of an overseer, and he was not necessarily moved by the same impulses as the master. He was often from the lowest social order in the community, commended chiefly by his business capacity, and separated by almost as wide a gulf from the rulers as the slave he directed, and on account of this ostracism inclined to be a greater tyrant toward those under him than he would otherwise have been. He was often an ex-servant or ex-slave, and not infrequently was himself a slave.[107]      As individuals, overseers often deserved better than to be included in the general opprobrium that was inseparably attached to their class, but they were not on the whole fitted to exercise justly and humanely the great powers of personal dominion committed to them by masters or assumed in their absence, without some ulterior check such as direct accountability to the master himself. Instances of violation of white female servants by negro overseers in the early days, and of negro females by white overseers were not unknown.[108]      The abuse of power by an overseer was restricted wherever he came under the master's personal supervision, which was the case in the majority of instances, as the absentee landowners and very large slave-holders were a comparatively small class. More than 55 per cent. of Virginia slaves of 1860

---

[106] Hening, III., 103, 460.
[107] Chastellux, *Travels*, II., 20; Olmstead, *Slave States*, 45.
[108] Robinson, *MSS.*, 256.

were held by owners of 1 to 20, and half of these by owners of
1 to 9. A poll of Spottsylvania County, Virginia, in 1783
showed 505 owners as possessing only 4,581 slaves, the largest
owner having but 159 slaves, nearly 50 per cent. having between one and five slaves, and only nine persons having over
forty. Twenty slaves were considered the minimum under an
overseer for a successful tobacco plantation, so the number of
plantations in the hands of single owners was necessarily restricted, as each required the use of some 1,000 acres of land.
The very small planters had a minimum of at least 200 acres,
requiring but four or five slaves, and even the holders of 5,000
or 6,000 acres had often only sufficient slaves to clear and
cultivate but a small proportion of their holdings. The population of the hilly and mountain regions was small slave-
holding, as it was mostly grain farming and grazing in occu-
pation as distinguished from planting; *i. e.*, following the
old custom of staple-crop raising.[109] The largest plantations
lay in the low country, mostly along the chief water courses,
the James, the Rappahanock, the York, the Potomac and the
inlets of Chesapeake Bay, just as farther south they were
along the Cape Fear, Santee, Savannah, Chattahoochee, Mobile,
Mississippi rivers, and the Mobile and other bays. Even
there the manor-houses and cultivated lands were quite a distance from each other, and the domain was in itself a petty
lordship under the rule and oversight of the master, so the
personal separation of master and slave in the prosperous days
of slavery in Virginia was not general but exceptional.

As the institution became less profitable economically or the
master acquired frontier lands, congestion was relieved by
removing the increase of slaves to their other lands, or by selling slaves to the domestic slave trader for the southern market, or by hiring and leasing them to corporations and indi-

[109] *Virginia Magazine of History and Biography*, January, 1897, 298;
*American Husbandman*, I., 231; Chastellux, *Travels*, 190, 191; Thatham,
*Agriculture of the United States*, 46, n.

viduals for a small net profit, either with or without lands and houses. This transfer from the direct control of the master might subject the dependent to harsh or barbarous treatment at the hands of persons who regarded him only with respect to his economic value. Masters were generally careful, both from interest and affection, to select good lessees where any choice existed. The tendency to develop harsh treatment under the lease system was restricted by penal and civil penalties, and in Jefferson's opinion slaves were more certain of better usage than when sold. The master's range of choice between humane and possibly cruel traders was more limited. Some traders were well known and respected all over the State, others locally, and many personally conducted their gangs down the Ohio and Mississippi to the cotton South. But once in the general market there was no security for the good usage of the slave until lodged with a humane master, except in the financial interest of the trader, which impelled him to keep his goods in the best condition for ready and profitable sale. It was the slave increase, however, that figured in this domestic slave trade, though not all of it. In 1840, regardless of the fact that Virginia was sending 6,000 surplus slaves annually to the Southwest, her slave population still increased by 5 per cent.[110]

The master's personal guardianship could not always follow his hired and leased slaves when they were sent to parts of the country far away from his domain, but if very harshly treated the slave had a legal remedy. It was customary to lease slaves not only with old plantations fully stocked and to persons beginning new ones, but for works of improvement in developing sections, such as the mines of the back country. These slaves usually came in large bodies from the eastern districts of the State, yet almost invariably, though in gangs which offered greater occasion for rigorous treatment, they

---

[110] Sparks, *Washington*, 1780, 263, *et seq.*; Smyth, *Travels*, I., 15; Jefferson, *Works*, IV., 342, 343, 416, 418.

were accorded great liberty and many privileges. They were allowed to visit their families and friends for Christmas on the old plantations, and might by harder work and odd jobs add considerable earnings of their own to what they gained for their master, and their full right to this wage of labor was not disputed. They often stipulated with their masters for a certain return and had the full enjoyment of all they might earn above this. In this way it was not unusual for them to save enough to purchase their freedom.[111]

The ordinary work of the male slave was praedial and that of the woman domestic, but it was not uncommon for women and children to work by the side of the men at the lighter tasks of field labor. In this their treatment differed from that of white female servants who were not ordinarily so employed. But the wives and mothers were at greater liberty than they are today, and the main duty of those not specifically household slaves was to take care of the quarters and the children while the hands were in the field. The life in the quarters was one of its own. There was much hospitality and sociability, much dancing, laughing, singing and banjo-playing when the day's work was done. This was the home of the plantation melody and clog dance. There was little that was morose or gloomy about the slave, either at work or rest. If his condition was deplorable it was rare that he recognized it to the extent of allowing it to affect his spirits. He was, under reasonable conditions, almost invariably cheerful, polite, and respectful to his superiors and strangers, without sycophancy and without fawning. He was well-bred like his master, and his manners were rather those of a person accustomed to liberty by the reign of law and order than to servile oppression. He often showed a dignity and self-respect that brought into striking contrast the pert inquisitiveness and false pride of the lowest stratum of the laboring whites in the North and the South, which proved so annoying and was so much com-

---

[111] Munford, *Reports*, III., 350; Olmstead, *Slave States*, 46, 47.

mented upon by foreign travelers. The field hand learned to improve his manners from the example of the whites, from the church and from those slaves above him who came in more direct contact with the best white society. Among these were the trusted body servant and nurse, the coach-driver, the butler, the purveyors, and the black aristocracy of skilled laborers—the carpenters, cobblers, and smiths—who were indispensable to every large plantation. Much free time was given them from their work,[112] often Saturday afternoon and always Sunday and the holidays of Easter, Whitsuntide and Christmas. The system of task-labor based on the slave of minimum capacity allowed much leisure or opportunity to the man above the average, often as much as one-fourth of his time. This he might employ to his own profit or pleasure within legal limits in travel, trade, and assembly or in acquiring property. The master's consent was rarely withheld to such free action of his slave at these times as was not actually menacing to others or likely to result in his own hurt. In sickness he had the same medical attention that came to the inmates of the great house; and often the skillful nursing and care of the mistress herself.[113]

Custom further allowed a distinct extension of the slave's right to private property. The use of small plots of ground adjoining their cabins was almost invariably allowed them. These were turned into gardens of flowers and truck, which might beautify the home or be disposed of to the slave's advantage. He was allowed to raise swine and frequently fowls, and might be given an old horse or mule by his master for the cultivation of his ground. An industrious slave might in this way lay aside a competence or even enough to purchase his freedom. Restrictions of the law had little effect upon the rights of user enjoyed by the slave or of property which was

---

[112] Hening, III., 103, 460; VI., 295; XI., 59; Randolph, *Reports*, VI., 672.

[113] Olmstead, *Slave States*, 101, 102, 109.

managed as *peculium*, but whose undivided profits the master allowed to go to his slave.[114]

The right to instruction, secular and religious, was based upon custom, but also enjoyed a legal sanction. Prior to 1805 it had been customary not only to provide instruction for slaves but for servants and free negroes. Church wardens and overseers of the poor upon binding out a bastard or a pauper child, black or white, specifically required that he should be taught to " read " and " write " and " calculate," as well as to follow some profitable form of labor.[115] The part played by free negroes in insurrections and the fear occasioned by a plot actually discovered at the time caused an enactment relieving authorities from the necessity of making such provisions for the future. And even the act of 1830–31 against unlawful assemblies put no check upon the gratuitous instruction of slaves nor upon the private instruction of free blacks by other colored persons.[116]

The education of the negro was designed to prepare him to take that place in economic, social, and political organization for which he seemed fitted under the slave *régime*. As a labor factor he found a place in general without competition already prepared in which he alone was master and had no superior. A single exception may be made in the field of local commerce and manufactures to which he was admitted. Here rather than in praedial labor he competed to the disadvantage of free labor. The navigation of his master's craft was almost wholly in his hands, and discouraged the increase of white seamen to such an extent that it was regarded a public evil, so a law of 1784 restricted the employment of slaves in river and bay navigation of tide water to one-third of the total persons so employed. In participation in domestic

---

[114] Adams, *View of Slavery*, 35, 49, 50.

[115] Statutes at Large, III., 124.

[116] Statutes at Large, 1804, 108; 1805, 124; 1831, 108; 1847, 120; Hurd, *Law of Freedom and Bondage*, II., 9.

manufactures he was not restricted legally nor to any extent by custom, when capacity was shown, but his presence was a serious discouragement to the growth of a free artisan class.[117]

Nor was the capacity of the minority of the colored race for higher education less vindicated under the old *régime* than under the new.    Instances of extraordinary intelligence among slaves and free negroes were common, and the facilities that some of these enjoyed for education would even now be considered remarkable.    Several examples are worthy of more than passing mention.    In the county court of Rockbridge in 1802 the freedom and character of a black, the Rev. John Chavis, were certified to and established beyond doubt by the court, which declared that he had passed " through a regular course of academic studies " as "a student at Washington Academy," now Washington and Lee University.    In the same region in 1820 a neighborhood school patronized by the whites consisted of thirty children, of whom ten were negroes.[118]    Probably the most interesting case in the entire South is that of an African preacher of Nottoway county, popularly known as " Uncle Jack," whose services to white and black were so valuable that a distinguished minister of the Southern Presbyterian Church felt called upon to memorialize his work in a biography.

Kidnapped from his idolatrous parents in Africa, he was brought over in one of the last cargoes of slaves admitted to Virginia and sold to a remote and obscure planter in Nottoway county, a region at that time in the backwoods and destitute particularly as to religious life and instruction.    He was converted under the occasional preaching of Rev. Dr. John Blair Smith, President of Hampden Sidney College, and of Dr. Wm. Hill and Dr. Archibald Alexander of Princeton, then young theologues, and by hearing the Scriptures read.    Taught by

---

[117] Hening, XI., 404.

[118] Dr. Wm. Henry Ruffner, *Rockbridge County News;* cf. Order Book, County Court, VI., 10, and *Lexington Gazette*, November 27, 1879.

his master's children to read, he became so full of the spirit and knowledge of the Bible that he was recognized among the whites as a powerful expounder of Christian doctrine, was licensed to preach by the Baptist church and preached from plantation to plantation within a radius of thirty miles, as he was invited by overseers or masters. His freedom was purchased by a subscription of whites and he was given a home and a small tract of land for his support. He organized a large and orderly negro church, and exercised such a wonderfully controlling influence over the private morals of his flock that masters, instead of punishing their slaves, often referred them to the discipline of their pastor, which they dreaded far more.

He stopped a heresy amongst the negro Christians of Southern Virginia by defeating in open argument a famous fanatical negro preacher named Campbell, who advocated noise and "the Spirit" against the Bible, winning over Campbell's adherents in a body. For over forty years, and until he was nearly a hundred years of age, he labored successfully in public and private amongst whites and blacks, voluntarily giving up his preaching in obedience to the law of 1832, the result of "Old Nat's War." Though assured that he would not be held under the penalty of the law, he refused to preach longer and expressed his full approval of it, saying with humility, "It is altogether wrong for such as have not been taught themselves to undertake to teach others. As to my preaching, I have long thought it was no better than the ringing of an old cow-bell and ought to be stopped." He believed in restraint as necessary for negroes, and said that the African Colonization Society would only succeed by applying these principles to the native Africans in their "superstitious and degraded condition." But for his age and time he might have anticipated the missionary work in Africa of another noble negro preacher, Rev. Mr. Shepherd, also a native of Virginia and a joint product of the post and antebellum methods of education. "Coming to the white man's country as a slave," said "Uncle Jack," "was the means of making me free in Christ Jesus," and "if I were only young enough I should rejoice to go back and preach the gospel to my poor countrymen. But it would be a great trial to live where there are no white people."

"Old Jack" understood and spoke English better than most negroes of the old days, because he read his Bible so constantly, and because he was admitted to the best society of his county. His pronunciation, style and choice of language were all good. He never used "massa" and "missus" for "master" and "mistress," nor "me" for "I," contrary to the general negro dialect. The most refined and aristocratic people paid tribute to him, and he was instrumental in the conversion of many whites. Says his biographer, Rev. Dr. Wm. S. White, "He was invited into their houses, sat with their families, took part in their social worship, sometimes leading the prayer at the family altar. Many of the most intelligent people attended upon his ministry and listened to his sermons with great delight. Indeed, previous to the year 1825 he was considered by the best judges, to be the best preacher in that county. His opinions were respected, his advice followed, and yet he never betrayed the least symptoms of arrogance or self-conceit. His dwelling was a rude log cabin, his apparel of the plainest and coarsest materials." This was because he wished to be fully identified with his class. He refused gifts of better clothes, saying, "These clothes are a great deal better than are generally worn by people of my color, and besides if I wear them I find I shall be obliged to *think about them even at meeting.*" [119]

Such indeed was the rare product of the old civilization as it is of the new. "Jack" was one of a thousand, yet he is an illustration of the fact that virtue had its own reward in the slave system, as well as in the free, and that there was no dis-

---

[119] White, *The African Preacher*, 5–139.

position to keep down deserving intelligence and morality whenever disclosed.

But the mass of negroes were not neglected, either socially or morally, as the ante-bellum type—now all too rapidly fading away—is an eloquent witness. The plantation of every pious man or woman had its Sunday school, taught by the devoted women of the household or by itinerant preachers who expounded the Bible and Christian doctrines to the circle of slaves, young and old, gathered around them. The domestics of the house and body servants were always summoned to partake in the sacred family worship and had their place around the hearthstone, in that inner, exclusive religious circle sanctified by holy memories and the historic custom of the race.[120]   In the towns and cities more specific means of religious instruction were provided. Separate Sunday schools for negroes, conducted by some of the foremost citizens of the locality or of the State, were organized with hundreds of attendants.   Such an one was that led by General Stonewall Jackson in the small town of Lexington while he was a professor in the Virginia Military Institute, and continued later by another of its professors, Colonel Preston.   Just after the Confederate victory at Manassas, when his fellow townsmen were waiting eagerly for news, Jackson wrote to Dr. White,

" *My dear Pastor,*—In my tent last night, after a fatiguing day's service, I remembered that I had failed to send you my contribution for our colored Sunday school.   Enclosed you will find my check for that object, which please acknowledge at your earliest convenience and oblige yours faithfully,

T. J. JACKSON."

Many of the negroes, free and slave, were members of the same churches as the whites.   A place was always set apart

---

[120] White, *The African Preacher*, 10, 14; Adams, *Southside View of Slavery*, 53, 56–58.

for them, either in the body or in the galleries of the church, which was peculiarly their own. Both by law and custom, at different times, they were required to attend service with the whites. The idea of "mixed" churches never troubled the slave-holder. The color line was political and social, not religious. In 1841, 500,000 southern slaves, one-fifth of their total number, were said to be church members, and 2,000,000 were regular attendants. Separate churches were sometimes built for them in the cities by the subscriptions of their masters, but the mass of negroes remained attached to the churches of the whites and departed from them slowly and reluctantly after the civil war.[121]

The strength of the personal attachment of the dependent for his superior and the supreme lesson of his teaching were never more strongly shown than in the trials of the war and reconstruction periods. When almost the total capable white population was absent in arms, when bands of marauders and camp sutlers followed the wake of victorious or retreating armies, devastating or appropriating what the soldiers had left, when their fears and avarice were appealed to from all sides by free negroes and disreputable whites, they were faithful almost to a unit, except the younger element, in devotion to their masters' implicit trust to their care of his family and property, protecting it even with their lives. They went into the war with "young master," they brought his body home, they helped the women to bury him, or they staid upon the lonely and devastated plantation, coaxing from its sterile soil, without the help of horse or plough, enough to keep together body and soul in the mistress, her children, and dependents.[122] That this was not due merely to physical and mental inertia or the habit of obedience from long restraint, the reluctance

[121] Campbell, *Race Problem in the South*, 13; cf. Mrs. Jackson's *Stonewall Jackson*, 181–182; Dabney, *Defense of Virginia*, 215, 217, 219.
[122] Campbell, *Race Problem*, 7; Burial of Latané; Acts, Called Session, 1862, 6; Acts, 1863, 38, 42; Dabney, *Virginia*, 293, 344.

with which many severed the tie and the frequent refusal to leave their old masters, no longer able to support or pay them, is sufficient proof. With many no change of relation was made, and the only evidence that slavery had ceased to exist was the regular wage which was paid where their former owner was able. The inefficient, the old, the sick still enjoyed the protection and support of the master who could give it, and when he could not, his sympathy and good offices in securing aid from the State. In truth, in custom the slave was not a slave, he was a servant. The term *slave* was unknown to common usage—it was a term of the law, and even there the relation was known as that of master and servant. He was often a retainer, a member of the family, a friend, though not equal to his chief. So in the manners of the people the tendency to continue or return to that earlier conception of dependent labor, servitude, from which legal slavery was evolved, was never wholly obliterated.

# CHAPTER III.

## MANUMISSION, EMANCIPATION, AND THE FREE MAN.

In the destruction as well as in the creation of the legal status of dependents in various forms of servitude much similarity exists. The three Roman Law modes of creating a slave—birth, capture, and condemnation on a criminal charge—were acknowledged in English and American law, but its three-fold mode of destroying this status by manumission and creating one of freedom was not so fully recognized. Emancipation with the Romans was the freeing of the child from the *patria potestas.* The process in the case of a daughter or a grandchild involved in the early Empire a single *mancipatio*, or solemn sale, and remancipatio, or re-sale by the vendee, and the *manumissio* of the father, which was the act of emancipation ; but in the case of a son the procedure was thrice gone through with before the manumission of the father completed the elaborate ceremony. Manumission required some solemn process of law or official act not only to protect the freedman in his new rights and as a check upon the master, but to acknowledge the supremacy of the state over such private acts of the individual as might affect the public weal. The master consequently admitted the freedom or declared his intent and desire to free his slave in a court of equity before the praetor, who in the name of the state assented to the manumission, or by will or trust demanded his enfranchisement according to the rules of law, or secured the entry of his name upon the register of citizens. Not until very late days was the formality of law and ceremony largely dispensed with. The power of the master in this respect, then, was subject to decided restriction and limitation. So also in English villainage, a closer analogue to American slavery, the lord in the early days could only free his man as respected himself, and third parties only as respected others, not the master; and enfranchisement required a formal process and legal sanction. Directly, it was made by a grant, a formal charter from the lord in consideration of the purchase of his freedom by another, and in later days even by the man himself, or at the pleasure of the lord without valuable consideration. But the lord could neither free nor transfer him by will. The indirect modes were by the suit of the villain based upon a manumission implied in a feoffment, convention or grant whose terms might be construed to acknowledge his freedom, or by non-user of his services for a year and a day, during which time he was a resident of privileged soil and treated as a freeman. These modes, suit and prescriptive right to freedom, were analogous to those of the creation of a villain, by prescription, long *usus* as a villain, and by acknowledgment of the status in a court of record, which acted as well as birth to establish unfree status.[1] These modes also, were finally applied to establish title to slaves in Virginia.

It is but natural, then, that, as custom and law but gradually sanctioned and defined the status of the unfree, so also the transition to a status of full freedom should be a development determined by changing conditions of economic and social demand, marked by a slow revolution of popular sentiment. As the definition of the full status of the slave covered a period of over two centuries in American history, so the rise of his descendant to the full rights and privileges of a state of freedom was and will be a continuing evolution conditioned chiefly upon his desert and ability to maintain that status or upon the power and assent of others to sustain him in it. Neither manumission nor emancipation could of itself vindicate perfect equality before the written and unwritten law of

---

[1] Vinogradoff, *Villainage*, 70, 86, 88, 184, 214, 275; Sohm, *Roman Law*, 25, 110, 393, 394.

the land or of society.   The ultimate tribunal in which this
progression was and is to receive its sanction is, by the nature
of society, self constituted in that power upon which rests the
constitutions of states themselves—Dominant Public Opinion
—the most equitable social judge of the rights of man.

If left to itself, emancipation—referring to a general movement, the elevation of the mass—rather than manumission,
the freeing of individuals, has been in many historic cases and
for best social and economic results should be gradual.   Yet
external force as a supposed or actual necessity to complete
such a social revolution has often been applied.   In many of
the American colonies and in Austria and Prussia, economic
forces were strong enough in themselves to effect the transition.
But in England, France, and part of Germany peasant wars,
partly social partly political, intervened to complete the
destruction of villainage and serfdom; and in America the
war of Secession left the enfranchised slave as but one of its
many results.   But both in England and in regions of the
South economic causes might have been sufficient to have
secured the same result, if left to long-continued and peaceful
action as at the North.[2]

The first step toward general emancipation, in both England
and Virginia, was in the growth of customary commutation
for service in rents; payments in kind or in money.   Through
this practice gradually arose upper or privileged classes, such
as the "molmen" and "gavelmen" of England, the house
and body servants of Virginia, the efficient artisans and the
aged, who tended to become peasant proprietors, or whose
service was viewed as based upon contract and custom, rather
than upon law.   This emancipation was *de facto* rather than
formal, but it was widespread, and influenced the elevation of
the whole dependent class toward the station of freemen, by
transferring a lower to a higher status through forms of service
and reverting, in America, from slavery to servitude.   Custom

---

[2] Tucker, *Progress of the United States*, 108–118.

found its ready response in legislation. Such a privileged dependent brought into the courts was almost certain to obtain his freedom either at once or after short duration, thus giving a further impetus to the public opinion that called for enfranchisement. Another form of commutation was that of service to the State in the master's stead. Here free services were by consent taken as presumptive evidence of free condition, and liberty consequently followed.[3]

Manumission began within a few years of enslavement. The effects of the act of baptism to free the slave, admitted by some, was legally denied in 1667, but a law in 1668, settling the question of the liability of the enfranchised to taxation, is witness to a class of free negro women at least at this early date. These, while allowed liberty, had not all of its privileges, as unlike white women they were still accounted tithables, though in cases of old age and merit they were exempted from taxation. So also in 1670 the manumission of male negroes and Indians was recognized, but they were not allowed like whites to hold Christian white servants, though they might have colored. The danger of the free negro and Indian element was very early recognized, and resulted, in 1691, in a restriction of the right of manumission. For fear that freedmen would harbor runaways, receive stolen goods, or from their age become a public charge it was determined by the Assembly, then passing an act to suppress "outlying slaves," to make transportation of ex-slaves without the colony a condition of the master's manumission. An exception to this was made in the case of especially meritorious public services, such as revealing conspiracies of negroes or law breakers, where a special act of assembly might intervene to give the slave all the rights of a free negro and choice of residence. This was done in the cases of Robert Ruffin's slave, Will, in 1710, at a cost of £40 to the State, and of Hinchia Marbury's slave, Kitt, at a cost of £1000 in 1779. The master's power

---

[3] Hening, XI., 308.

to manumit was not further restricted by law until 1723, when in consequence of insurrections freedom was limited upon such meritorious service as was "adjudged and allowed by the governor and council" and the "license" of the master obtained therefor.[4]  Manumission by special act of assembly upon the master's application, sometimes naming a number of slaves at one time, however, continued as a regular mode until the growth of testamentary manumission.  In 1729 there was a curious case of a negro's obtaining his freedom for revealing an herb medicine by which wonderful cures had been effected.

The origin of the recognition of manumission by will is interesting.  It was due to a necessity that arose from the American Revolution.  Lord Dunmore, the royal governor, having withdrawn from the government of Virginia, it was impossible at the time to obtain the consent of the governor and council to manumission, as provided by law, so that one John Barr, having no other recourse, added a codicil to his will freeing two female slaves and creating a trust in land and property in their behalf.  Upon Barr's death in 1777 the will was contested, but the Assembly passed a special act confirming it and the manumission, but declared that it established no precedent except for exactly similar cases.  Many of these, however, probably arose during the Revolution.  After the war manumission was fully established, not only as to wills but as to any written and sealed instrument acknowledged or proved and made a matter of record in the county court, by the act of 1782, which stated that emancipation was "judged expedient under certain restrictions."[5]  These were that the liberator should be responsible for the support of imbecile, disabled, superannuated and minor slaves, else they would have been generally liberated to their own and the State's disadvan-

---

[4] Hening, II., 260, 267, 280; III., 536; IV., 133; X., 115; XI., 308; General Court Records, 1670, October 4, p. 21.

[5] Hening, IX., 320, 321; X., 221, 372; XI., 39; *Virginia MSS.*, B. R. O., 1729, June 29.

tage. The impulse given to manumission by will and by deed under the operation of this act, is shown by the yearly manumissions, averaging over 1,000 for the next ten years. Tucker estimates that 2,800 free negroes probably existed in 1782, but the census shows their number to have increased to 12,866 in 1791. They were more than were to be found in the whole of New England, and but 1,087 less than in New York, New Jersey, and Pennsylvania together. By an act of 1783 manumission was extended to include even verbal promises by masters of freedom for service in arms in their stead where the free service was rendered. In 1787 two special acts recognized the validity of manumissions by devise prior to 1782. They enforced the provisions of wills, made in 1778 and 1780, freeing a number of slaves, on the ground that it was deemed "just and proper" that the "benevolent intentions" of the testators should be carried into effect.[6]

General manumission by will or deed prior to 1782 could only be sustained legally where its effect was limited upon the future contingency of assent of the Assembly or of the legalizing of this mode. By the liberal construction of the courts and Assembly in such cases, however, many slaves obtained their freedom. Some wills wisely provided also for conditional manumission to take effect after a period of years, varying from majority to thirty years, creating a trust for the testator's relatives or heirs, in order to prepare the slaves by instruction for the proper enjoyment of liberty. Progressive manumission of the children of females, and of their children born before the age limit was reached, often carried the execution of the will over long periods and beyond the ordinary limitation of chattel remainders, but the trustees enjoyed no profits except the use of the slave, and the chancellor attempted to have even this profit returned to the slave. Devises in favor of charity and particularly those in favor of liberty were liberally construed, so a devise made by a Quaker in 1781 of

---

[6] Tucker, *Slavery*, 72 and note; *Blackstone*, 66; Hening, XII., 611, 613.

his slaves to the yearly meeting to be manumitted was held good on account of the well known attitude of the Quakers toward slavery.   Likewise a deed which freed a female slave, reserving the right to her issue as slaves, was voided as to the *reservation* and the woman and children freed.   In manumission, however, widows' dower and creditors' interests had to be protected, and freed slaves might be taken or reduced to servitude for a term of years to satisfy the obligations.[7]

The courts regarded the legacy of freedom a specific legacy so the freed slave came into the hands of the executor, and could not be touched without his assent, and the executor commonly discharged any indebtedness from other means or hired out the slaves till the debt was paid before he freed them. Deeds of manumission were admitted with great laxity by the courts.   Writing of the testator was regarded sufficient proof, though the deed had never been acknowledged or recorded and no witness was present to establish it.   Non-cupative wills were admitted.   Only a single case of a possibly strained construction and unjust decision by the court, defeating the plain intent of several wills, is on record, and this holding was opposed by the opinion of the legal profession in Virginia, and the principle was reversed in other decisions.   A testator loaned slaves to his wife for life, provided that on her death they be given the choice of freedom or slavery.   Freedom was denied on the ground that the condition of slavery was one of absolute civil incapacity and a slave could not legally choose.   Wills also frequently contained legacies for emancipated slaves, but a will which attempted to provide for care, tuition, and wages for a slave and issue, intending to create a condition midway between slavery and freedom, would not be sustained.[8]

---

[7] Call, *Reports*, II., 270, 292; V., 311, 330; Randolph, *Reports*, IV., 599; Hening and Munford, *Reports*, I., 519; Grattan, *Reports*, XIV., 333.

[8] Leigh, *Reports*, V., 252, 289; VII., 691; Gratton, *Reports*, II., 227; XIV., 138, 139; Minor, *Institutes*, I., 187.

Several modes of obtaining freedom through the action of statutory law existed. Until 1794 slaves imported, sold or bought contrary to the act of 1778 declaring the importation of slaves illegal, were made free. An act of 1785 designating who were slaves declared, "Slaves which shall hereafter be brought into this commonwealth and kept therein one whole year together, or so long at different times as shall amount to one year, shall be free." This applied even to Virginia slaves sold or transported into another State and resold or retransported into Virginia. Such cases arose with slaves removed to Maryland and Massachusetts. A Massachusetts man came to Virginia and married a women owning two slaves. In 1797 he removed to Boston, intending to live there, but as by the Massachusetts Constitution slaves could not legally be held there he came back in the following year to Virginia, and held these slaves till they discovered in 1828 that they had a legal action for freedom. When reënacted in 1792 this act made an exception of Alexandria County in the District of Columbia.[9]

By the act of 1795 a very great boon was given to the slave in the simplification of the precedure in a suit for freedom. A slave was allowed to sue *in forma pauperis.* He made his complaint to a local magistrate or court, who required the owner to give bond to allow his slave to come to the next court to maintain suit. If he refused the slave was taken into custody by the State, at the master's expense, to protect him, counsel was assigned, process was issued against the owner and the slave had free writs of subpoena, attended the taking of depositions, and might come and go freely in the prosecution of his suit. A suit might be instituted even without petition to the court. The same strictness of form was not required as in other actions, irregular issues even were sustained, and great liberality was shown by the Court of Appeals in the

---

[9] Hurd, *Law of Freedom*, II., 2, 4, 5; Call, *Reports*, V., 425; Leigh, *Reports*, V., 615; Statutes at Large, III., 76.

cases that came to it.   Technical variations in the evidence
from the bill were not noted, and decision followed equitable
rather than legal rights.   Cases were not postponed, except for
evidence, but came up regularly in the first quarterly district
court.[10]

In some suits for freedom the courts held that the burden of
proof lay upon the slave; in others, particularly in cases of
importation after 1786, freedom was assumed upon *prima facie*
or presumptive evidence.   The suer for freedom might elect
his own court and the case was given preference, being tried
without regard to its place on the docket, and, without the formality of pleading, a jury was impanneled to try it.   In case
of detention of the slave during suit damages could be awarded
him.   In other suits a negro suing for freedom also was treated
as a free negro.   All suits proceeded without cost to the slave.
In order to further protect the man in his right to liberty, certificates of freedom were required as early as 1776.   A registry of free negroes and mulattoes, as well as of dower and
life-estate slaves, in which the facts and circumstances of the
manumission and a description of the person were entered, was
after 1803 and 1804 kept in every county.   This registry was
of great value in preventing illegal detention of ex-slaves and
unjust suits for freedom, protecting thus the rights of both
masters and slaves.   A suit for freedom might be maintained
by a slave sent or hired out of the State by his master if the
State to which he went was a free State, but if it was not and
the master resided or owned lands in the State his right to the
slave was not infringed.   Under the common law, as it did not
acknowledge the institution of slavery, a slave might be
released from his master's control by writ of *habeas corpus,*
even though a temporary sojourner in a country where slavery
was not recognized.   But if the slave domiciled again with

---

[10] Tucker, *Slavery,* 73, note; Statutes at Large, n. s., II., 19, 79; Washington, *Reports,* I., 306; Hening and Munford, *Reports,* I., 145; Randolph
*Reports,* IV., 136, 466.

the master the rights of the master were not impaired. If the slave went away or escaped without the master's consent to a non-slave-holding jurisdiction he could be reclaimed, prior to fugitive slave acts,[11] only by express arrangement. The federal fugitive slave law of 1793 protecting a master's right, and that of 1850 employing the machinery of government for the restoration of his property were of practical value chiefly in arresting the growth of facilities for absconding.

To protect an imported slave in his right to liberty under the provisions of the act of 1786 was not always easy, as by movement from place to place during a year's time the proof of the identity of the slave might be lost; so in 1793 an act was passed requiring justices of the peace who had notice of importations of slaves, directly or indirectly, from Africa or the West Indies to transport them immediately out of Virginia. In the session of 1805 and 1806 the principle of the act of 1691 was revived, and no slave emancipated after the 1st of May, 1806, could legally remain in Virginia after becoming of age. In 1819 this was so far mitigated that the county court might grant leave to slaves of good character, " sober, peaceful, orderly and industrious," to remain in the State; but such permission granted to a female did not include her issue and the court might revoke its leave for cause shown. This act was incorporated in the third constitution of Virginia in 1851, and any slave, except one freed by will prior to the act or permitted to remain, forfeited his liberty after twelve months, and might be seized and sold by the overseers of the poor for the benefit of the poor. So also any slave brought in, sold, or hired for a year, was not freed, but his title vested in the overseers of the poor, and as a discouragement a severe penalty was laid upon the person bringing such a slave into

---

[11] Tucker, *Blackstone*, I., pt. II., appendix, 48; Acts of Assembly, 1819, 436; 1826, 25; 1830, 107; 1836, 47; Leigh, *Reports*, VI., 607; Constitution, 1851, sec. 20; Randolph, *Reports*, VI., 67; Statutes, 1806, January 25; 1807, January 12.

Virginia. The slaves and servants of travellers and commercial men were exempted from this provision in 1807. In 1812, slave-holders coming from other States to reside in Virginia might under some restrictions bring in slaves, not for sale, provided they would within three months afterwards export a female slave between the ages of ten and thirty years for every slave they imported. The evident intent of this act was to check the natural increase of slaves. The restrictions upon slave importation were not even partially removed until 1819, and decided limitations continued until 1860. It was the menace of the free negro element that chiefly caused these restrictions upon importation and manumission and the tardy growth of the sentiment of general emancipation. An act of 1793 attempted to prevent the immigration of free negroes and mulattoes by imposing the penalty of £100 on the person bringing them in, and by making the negroes liable to seizure and removal to the place whence they came, by any citizen, at the cost of the importer. In 1860 the General Assembly was empowered to enforce restrictions upon manumission and to provide laws for the relief of the commonwealth by removing the free negro element. The Assembly was not allowed hereafter to emancipate any slave or descendant of a slave.[12]

The proper disposal of the free negro, a question which, dependent upon the large proportion of blacks to whites, was peculiar to Virginia and the South and of small consequence in the North, retarded all movements for general emancipation. The earlier and later advocates of enfranchisement, men of the greatest wisdom and patriotism like Jefferson, Tucker, and Randolph, all thought that schemes of emancipation were merely chimeras or would inflict a more serious social and political injury than slavery itself, unless the free negro element was successfully removed from the limits of the State. As Jefferson affirmed, mixture with the freedman socially and

---

[12] Code, 1814, II., 126; Revised Code, 1819, I., 421, 422; Code, 1849, 457, 749; 1860, 511; Statutes at Large, n. s., I., 239.

in blood raised an issue new to the question of slave emancipation on a large scale. The racial difference of the negro and the Indian, with its distinction in color and faculty, was considered a stain to the blood, the beauty and the dignity of the white race, so that as freedom enhanced the danger of this mixture freedmen must be removed beyond its remotest possible realization. This fear on the part of philanthropists, together with the avarice of the mean, Jefferson thought were the greatest obstacles to emancipation.

A strong sentiment even amongst the people, however, for general emancipation several times showed itself, and but for the unfortunate reaction produced by outside interference the cause of freedom might possibly have triumphed in the Assembly of 1831–32. In the preamble of an amending act of 1794, providing an easy mode for the recovery of freedom by slaves illegally detained, complaint was made against voluntary associations of individuals who, affecting to render "justice toward persons unwarrantably held in slavery," were assuming the duties of the government and involving masters in "unfounded law suits," or illegally depriving them of their property and causing "great and alarming mischiefs in other States" which might spread to Virginia.[13] Consequently, a ready method of conducting suits of freedom was devised and a penalty of $200 laid upon any one who forged an instrument declaring or promising freedom to slaves. A further act in 1798 disqualified members of such societies as jurors in suits for freedom.[14] Thus early was manifested that jealousy and fear of outside interference and abolition sentiment that helped to defeat schemes of general emancipation in Virginia.

Some of the first attempts at manumission by will came from the Quakers. In 1771 John Pleasants, a Quaker, made a manumitting will which came to probate in 1800, and for

---

[13] Jefferson, *Notes on Virginia*, 213, 214; Howison, *Virginia*, II., 439; Revised Code, 1814, I., 485, 486.

[14] Statutes at Large, n. s., II., 77.

some time prior to 1781 a Quaker society "had been anxiously endeavoring," said Judge Lyons of the Court of Appeals in 1804, "to procure an enabling statute for that purpose from the legislature." The effort was no doubt instrumental in securing the act for manumission by will. A sentiment favorable to emancipation then existed among certain classes, a minority, from quite an early time. It was Jefferson who first gave effective and forcible expression to this sentiment. His views upon the dangers of both the slave and the free negro elements—as upon most subjects to which he gave earnest thought—deserved and received the careful attention of his contemporaries. He disliked the institution of slavery intensely on account of both social and political effects which he either saw around him or thought he foresaw.[15] "There must doubtless be," he says in 1781, "an unhappy influence on the manners of our people produced by the existence of slavery amongst us. The whole commerce between master and slave is a perpetual exercise of the most boisterous passions, the most unremitting depotism on the one part and degrading submission on the other. Fathers give way before the children —children see their passions and learn to imitate them, give loose to the worst of passions, and daily exercised in tyranny cannot but be stamped by it with odious peculiarities." Jefferson said that slavery not only destroyed the best morals of a people but their industry also, affirming, "A very small proportion of proprietors are ever seen to labor." The key to the apparent fervor and extravagance of his language, which became so intense, as he proceeded to discuss the question in his "Notes," that he perforce breaks off, admitting himself that he cannot pursue the subject "with temperance," is to be found in the doctrines of his political creed and philosophy. "With what execrations," he says, "should statesmen be loaded" who permit "one-half of the citizens to trample upon the rights of the other, transform those into despots and these into enemies,

---

[15] Call, *Reports*, V., 330 ; Ford, *Jefferson*, II., 266.

destroy the morals of one part and the *amor patriæ* of the
other," who cannot call that his native country "in which he
is born to live and labor for another," but must "lock up all
the faculties of his nature—and entail his own miserable condition on the endless generations proceeding from him." And
further, he asserts that the only firm basis of the liberties of a
nation is "the conviction in the people's mind that their
liberties are the gift of God," and "slavery removes this conviction." He trembled for his country when he thought of the
wrath of God against this unjust violation of the natural
rights of man. "God is just—his justice cannot sleep for
ever," he says, "considering numbers, nature and natural
means only an exchange of situation between oppressor and
oppressed is possible" and "by supernatural interference"
probable. "The Almighty has no attribute which can take
side with us in such a contest—considerations of policy, of
history, natural and civil," advocate a change. Jefferson's
denunciation was against slavery not only as an abstract but
as a practical principle. It was sinful *per se*, and logically
because of this its fruits were those of unrighteousness. He
wrote for French ears attuned to doctrines of equality and to
the theory of the rights of man, and in some pique, too per-
haps, at not being able to convince his fellow-citizens that the
practice of slavery was wrong, however wrong its theory.[16]

But he had a hearing even in Virginia. St. George Tucker,
Professor of Law in William and Mary College, and a judge
of the General Court of Virginia, felt like Jefferson, that
slavery was "incompatible with the principles of our government and that of the Revolution." "We were imposing," he
says, "on a fellow man who differed in complexion from us,
a slavery ten times more cruel than the utmost extremity of
those grievances and oppressions of which we complained.
It is time," he adds, in 1796, "that we should admit the
evidence of moral truth and learn to regard them as our fellow

---

[16] Jefferson, *Notes on Virginia*, in Ford III., 244, 267.

9

men and equals except in those particulars where accident or possibly nature may have given us some advantage." Madison, Washington, and Henry were more conservative, but wished to see the abolition of slavery. Madison opposed the admission into the Constitution of the idea of property in human beings. This of all times was the time when the slavery question should have been settled. Washington said, "It is among my first wishes to see some plan adopted by which slavery may be abolished by law." Henry wrote in 1773 to a Quaker friend, "It [slavery as a principle] is as repugnant to humanity as it is inconsistent with the Bible and destructive of liberty. Every thinking honest man rejects it in speculation, but how few in practice from conscientious motives. . . . I am drawn along by the general inconvenience of living without them. I will not, I cannot, justify it." Before the close of the Revolution Jefferson thought he saw a distinct change of popular sentiment. "The Spirit of the master is abating." he writes, "that of the slave rising from the dust, his condition is mollifying, the way I hope preparing under the auspices of heaven for a total emancipation, and this is disposed in the order of events to be with the consent of the masters rather than by their extirpation." But none of the leaders, apologists or anti-slavery men, had a remedy to offer adequate to the disease, and a favorable popular sentiment, which might have sustained a change promising success, languished for nearly half a century longer till finally quenched by jealousy of outside interference.[17]

Three well-defined plans for a gradual general emancipation were publicly presented in Virginia. They were all based upon a two-fold principle: (1) emancipation only of slaves born after a certain future time, especially females; and (2) removal of the free colored population beyond the limits of the United States. The first provision was necessary to pro-

---

[17] Tucker, *Blackstone*, App., 55; Adams, *South-Side View of Slavery*, 106; Ford, *Jefferson*, II., 267; Bancroft, *United States*, VI., 416, 417.

tect vested interests, the second to protect society in the other States. This would not have been possible if the progressive emancipation of some northern States had been adopted, as it both permitted the residence of free blacks and encouraged their sale by natural economic law to the slave States prior to emancipation. The prevention of this latter effect as to surrounding slave States in the South could only reasonably be looked for in the simultaneous application of similar plans there or in laws against slave importations. The burden might have been shifted gradually from State to State till it was removed from the borders of the Union, but such a plan would not commend itself to either just or practical men. The notion of freeing the whole body of southern or northern slaves at once without Federal intervention and compensation was regarded as absurd by all thinking men North and South until the rise of the abolitionists. In 1824, forty-five years after suggesting his plan, Jefferson wrote to Jared Sparks, " I have never been able to conceive any other practicable plan." The idea of freeing one and a half millions of slaves in the United States and of sending off the whole body at once " nobody conceives to be practicable for us nor expedient for them. As property they are lawfully vested and cannot be taken away." To buy them he thought was too expensive. Valued at $200 each it would require $600,000,000 to absolve the master's claims, and to this must be added the cost of transportation and of implements to establish them in independence, some $300,000,000 more. The total final cost would not be less than $36,000,000 a year for twenty-five years, so he declares, " It cannot be done in this way," but we must " emancipate the after born." Valuing the infant at $12.50, he hoped to reduce the property cost to $37,500,000.[18]

With such sentiments Jefferson, as one of the committee appointed by the first Assembly of the Commonwealth to revise the whole code of Virginia and to purge it of all " prin-

---

[18] Randolph, *Memoirs of Jefferson*, IV., 388, *et seq.*

ciples inconsistent with Republicanism," had outlined a plan which was reported to the legislature in 1779 together with the joint work of Wythe and Pendleton on the code. The proposition was put forward as an amendment to the bill of laws and was to be offered when the bill was taken up. Tucker states, however, that for some reason, not certainly known, the measure was not brought forward in the Assembly, "possibly," he suggests, "because objections were foreseen to that part of the bill which related to the disposal of the blacks after they had attained a certain age." The plan was to emancipate all slaves born after the passage of the act. They were to remain with their parents till a certain age and then to be educated at public expense in "tillage, arts or sciences"' until of age, which was 18 years for females and 21 years for males. They were then to be colonized in "such place as the circumstances of the time should render most proper," to be furnished with "arms, implements, seeds, pairs of useful domestic animals and household implements," and to be declared "a free and independent people" under "our alliance and protection" until strong enough to stand alone. The displacement of labor thus caused was to be remedied by the importation of "an equal number of whites sent for by vessels to other parts of the world."

To deal with the free negro question as the United States has since seen fit to do was in Jefferson's opinion the height of folly. It was futile to hope to "retain and incorporate the blacks into the state." "Deep rooted prejudices of the whites, ten thousand recollections of blacks of injuries sustained, new provocations, the real distinction nature has made and many other circumstances will divide us," he predicts, "into parties and produce convulsions which will probably never end but in the extermination of one or the other race." Amalgamation he regarded as both revolting and socially impossible. He felt the black was too far the inferior of the white in physical and mental qualities, though, strange to say, he defended his morals. No place was suggested for the colony, but he secretly hoped one would open up in "the revolutionary state of America then commenced." [19]

This hope he thought was realized in 1824 in independent St. Domingo under the control of blacks, who were willing to receive the freedmen as citizens and to pay the cost of transportation. The chief expense thus left was the rearing of infants, which he suggested might be borne by appropriations from the vacant lands "ceded [to the United States] by the very States now needing relief." The property loss now involved amounted to only half of the direct taxes annually continued for twenty-five years, and this would be gradually lessened for the next twenty-five years, which would mark its final extinction. "And this amount," he urged, "was paid not in cash, but by the delivery of an object which the Virginians had never known nor computed as a part of their property, and those who did not possess it would be called on for nothing." "Who could estimate," he says of this project, "its blessings! I leave this to those who will live to see its accomplishment and to enjoy a beatitude forbidden to my age, but I leave it with this admonition, to arise and be doing." The notion of the master meeting the State half way and compromising upon a mutual property sacrifice was afterwards taken up by Faulkner, who held that the State had a right to destroy property in slaves, and also by McDowell, who urged a like principle against Goode in the debate of 1831–32. [20]

Tucker, Jefferson's contemporary, felt like him that Divine Providence would aid and smile upon the emancipation of slaves. "But human prudence forbids," he says, "that we should engage in a work of such hazard as a general and simultaneous emancipation." "Immediate emancipation" to him meant "immediate and general famine," which the products of all the other States even could not relieve, for south

---

[19] Ford, *Jefferson*, II., 242, 245; Tucker, *Slavery*, 73.

[20] Randolph, *Memoirs of Jefferson*, IV., 388, *et seq.*; Faulkner's Speech, 14–16; *Richmond Whig*, March 24, 1832.

of Delaware there was a slave population of nearly 650,000, which was more than half the white population, while in agricultural labor there were four slaves to every free white man. The question was thus more similar to that in the French West Indies than to that in Massachusetts, where the proportion of whites to blacks was sixty-five to one. The other difficulty was the future of the negroes themselves. They must be prepared for their future condition. To expel them all at once from the United States meant "lingering death by disease," or as natural "idlers" and "profligates" they would be exposed to the misery of an insufficient subsistence. The plan he proposed in 1796 was to effect the "abolition of slavery without emancipating a single slave." He objected to Jefferson's colonization scheme on the ground of the expense, which was five times greater than the annual revenue of Virginia, and on the ground of the incapacity of "hordes of vagabonds, robbers, and murderers in their still savage state and debased "condition" to govern themselves. If colonized in the United States internal warfare or Indian hostility would extirpate them, if outside, their destruction as invaders was almost as certain. To incorporate them into the body politic was a menace to the whites, and an impossibility. Some middle course had to be found, he urged, between the "tyrannical and iniquitous policy" which held "so many human creatures in a state of grievous bondage and that which would turn loose a numerous starving and enraged banditti upon the innocent descendants of their former oppressors."

Tucker's plan, consequently, was partly made up from Jefferson's and partly from those of other States. It provided that after the adoption of the plan, (1) every female born and her issue should be free, but should remain with the family as servants for twenty-eight years and then receive appropriate freedom dues for a start of life, being treated during their servitude in all respects as white servants and apprentices; (2) civil slavery should be retained, and officeholding, action as an attorney, juror or witness except in cases between blacks, franchises, or interests in lands greater than a twenty-one-year lease should be prohibited. And further the emancipated were not to keep or bear arms, except under legal limitations; nor to marry a white; nor to be an executor or administrator; nor to be capable of making a will or acting as a trustee; nor of maintaining any real action, but they were to be tried in criminal cases as free negroes and mulattoes were at that time entitled to be. This provision was a compromise to prejudice, but with a distinct object. The privileges were to be enlarged as occasion demanded, and the personal rights and property of the servants, though limited, were to be protected by law. "By denying them," said Tucker, "the most valuable privileges which civil government affords I wish to render it their interest to seek those privileges in some other climate." He seems to have had Spanish territory in view, and hoped the cutting off of ambition, power of resentment, and landed property would be sufficient to induce emigration as a substitute for colonization.

His plan was based upon a deduction from Jefferson's theory of inalienable rights and natural equality, that no property could exist in an unborn child. "The right of one man over another," he said, "is neither founded in nature nor in sound policy. It cannot extend to those not in being. No man can be deprived of what he doth not possess." He estimated that no male would be fully emancipated for 45 years and that it would take over a century to complete the process. Not for forty years would slave population diminish; on the contrary for thirty years it would increase, and after sixty years one-third of the number of then-existing slaves would remain, while the bound blacks under twenty-eight years of age would equal the original number of slaves.[21] The plan was elaborated and published, together with a dissertation upon slavery, in the appendix to his commentaries on Black-

---

[21] Tucker, *Blackstone*, Appendix, pt. II., Vol. I., 68, 72, 75, 79.

stone, and as a separate pamphlet in 1796; but although widely read it bore no fruit. The time was not yet, and the proposed disposition of the negro element, as was the case with Jefferson's plan, was sufficient to defeat its acceptance. It is interesting that he looked for the natural abolition of slavery through the form by which it naturally arose, servitude. This was both logical and possible if the emigration of the freedmen would have been forced by the restrictions and economic law, but this was the doubtful feature.

Many Virginians on the failure of these plans turned their hopes toward the project of the African Colonization Society, the establishment of the colony of Liberia, and lent their earnest support to insuring its successful inception and continuance. Many slaves were manumitted by their owners on the promise that they would become colonists, and many more were freed by will on this specific condition. In some cases they refused this alternative and chose to remain slaves rather than be deported to Africa. Some even escaped from the decks of vessels leaving Baltimore and made their way back to Virginia to become slaves. The success of the colonization movement which finally resulted in the formation of the African Colonization Society was largely due to the suggestions and aid of Jefferson, Monroe, Mercer, Randolph, Bushrod Washington and other Virginians, supported by several acts of the State Legislature from 1800 to 1816. It was through Monroe at the instance of Robert Goodloe Harper that the society received Federal countenance and became a general instead of a local movement. It represented a southern as well as a northern movement toward emancipation, combining with the Christianization of Africans a step toward the solution of the negro problem. Maryland, Virginia, and North Carolina were not behind other States like New York and Pennsylvania in direct aid or encouragement through State societies. An act of the Virginia Legislature in 1850 appropriated $30,000 annually for five years to transport free negroes to Liberia through the Virginia Colonization Society.

In 1853 a colonization board was appointed, with a like appropriation for five years, to be raised by bequests and a tax of $1 each on free negroes between twenty-one and forty-five years old. Even in later years, after the war, Virginia gave one of her bravest soldiers, the Rt. Rev. Charles Clifton Penick, to labor efficiently as a missionary and Episcopal Bishop among these freedmen at Cape Palmas, and not least among the presidents of the Republic of Liberia was a Virginia-born slave, James S. Payne.[22]

The third plan for emancipation, distinctly formulated and proposed in the Virginia Assembly of 1831–32, was that of Thomas Jefferson Randolph, a nephew of Jefferson. It was a result of the exciting circumstances surrounding the insurrection of Nat Turner. Says Dew in his review of the famous debate on the subject that year: "Consternation and dismay all through the State—rumors of disaffections, plots and insurrections and even of massacres, frightened the timid and occasioned in the minds of many even in the lower parts of Virginia anxiety to remove this monstrous evil. Plans for partial and total emancipation were earnestly pressed upon the attention of the legislature." "Never before," he says, "had the subject of emancipation been seriously discussed in any of the legislatures of our Southern slave-holding country." Some persons looked to the Colonization Society. Some were disposed to strike at the root of the evil and to call upon the General Government to extirpate slavery. "But State pride," he continues, "could not be a suppliant to a General Government whose unconstitutional action she had ever been foremost to resist." A resort to the legislature of the State was at last forced. "The Legislature," he says, "was composed of an unusually large number of young and inexperienced men," and this, together with the fact that "no enlarged wise or practical plan of operations was proposed by the abolitionists,"

---

[22] McPherson, *Liberia*, Johns Hopkins University Studies, 16–19, 31–33, 53–59; Acts, 1849–50.

contributed toward defeat. The debate, however, was eloquent and long sustained, a great number of speakers appearing in it, and "day after day multitudes thronged the Capital" to hear the speeches. The Assembly "in its zeal for the discussion set aside all prudential considerations," such as the possible effect of incendiary utterances that might make the slave believe his lot one of injustice and cruelty and so give him the excuse of a revolt, or might encourage further aggressions by northern abolitionists. "Regardless of this," says Dew, "the Assembly openly and publicly debated the subject before the world" and the whole matter was submitted to a thorough discussion. All seemed to be perfectly agreed in the necessity of removal in case of emancipation. Three propositions were brought forward: (1) Deportation of the whole mass to Africa was urged by the members of the lower counties—it might be there made a means of Christianizing the heathen. The objections raised to this were first, cost—slaves representing one-third of the wealth of the State and half that of lower Virginia, and, valued at $200 each, would require a first outlay of $94,000,000—and second, the claim that land values depended on slavery; (2) Deportation and colonization in Africa of the increase only—which at that time was about 6,000 a year—was proposed by those who thought the profit of selling slaves to the Southwest was an encouragement to the retention of the system. This of course would find no general support, as value and transportation would cost the State $1,380,000, a year while the domestic slave trade accomplished the same result as far as removal was concerned without cost; (3) The plan proposed by Randolph.[23] This not only denied the master's property right according to the principle *partus sequitur ventrem*, but put upon him the obligation of raising and maintaining the child till of age at eighteen or twenty-one years. The assumption was that the labor of the child after

---

[23] Dew, *Review of the Debate of* 1832, Madison Pamphlets, Vol. XIV., 6, 8, 47, *et seq.*

twelve or fourteen years would offset the cost of the preceding years. The proposition was to emancipate all born after 1840 and that the freedman should earn and pay his own transportation from America. To do this he was to be hired out after becoming of age till he accumulated enough for his passage. The plan was harshly criticized. Dew says, " Scarcely any of the legislature, we believe not even the author himself, entirely approved of this plan."

The failure of the Virginia advocates of emancipation to agree and to combine for any length of time upon a single definite or practicable plan strengthened the forces of their opponents and caused their final defeat by a small majority. Will was not wanting, but method unhappily was. The effect of this failure was to create the feeling among the people of Virginia that the negro, slave or free, was an incubus, hopelessly irremovable; and on the part of northern abolitionists, now in the first freshness of their zeal, an aggressiveness that inflamed resentment in Virginia and prevented a future calm consideration of the problem.

To many the debate had shown the slow progress of Virginia in population, "an unerring symptom," says Dew, "of her want of prosperity and the inefficacy of slave labor." It was held that slave labor could no longer be truly profitable except in cotton, sugar, rice and such crops. It shut out manufactures and profitable immigration, while it was causing the emigration of some of the best elements of Virginia's population to new lands in the West and South. White emigration had reached an average of 3000 persons a year by 1830. This symptom of over-density of blacks, now for the first time generally recognized, had become so marked in the next ten years that George Tucker, a professor of Philosophy and Political Economy in the University of Virginia, from an extended study of the census reports, predicted the early extinction of slavery in Maryland and Virginia and the final progress of extinction Southward based upon economic causes alone, chiefly that of the relation of a dense immobile population to land and subsistance. The distinguished Bishop Meade, of the Episcopal Church, in 1857 went even further in denunciation of the effects of slavery.[24] After fifty years of observation and thirty years travel over the State, conversing with the most intelligent Virginians, he gave as his opinion that slavery injured Virginia's religious, political, and agricultural interests. "Notwithstanding," he says, "the cruelties accompanying the African slave trade, the advantage of it has been on the side of the negro temporally and spiritually, [yet] wasteful agriculture and consequent emigration must be admitted. Large estates cultivated by slaves prevented the establishment of villages, churches, and schools," and "produced in many sons of Virginia gentlemen the feeling that labor was a disgrace." But he continues, "among the upper classes, there is far more academic and collegiate education in Virginia than in any other State, and slavery brings out more good feelings than bad." As to emancipation, he said that if it was more to the negroes' good than to their masters' injury he was sure God would reveal it. Such was the sentiment of the well informed.

Arguments advanced against slavery itself rather than for the protection of society, though presented in the debate of 1831–32, had but a limited recognition. As to the fear of insurrection even, it was urged that no place in the world was more secure than Virginia, that in the country generally houses were left open at night. The ethical and political arguments based upon Jefferson and Montesquieu were denied and easily refuted to the full satisfaction of the pro-slavery men of the Assembly. Such arguments, frequently advanced by northern anti-slavery leaders, would have been condemned for that alone if for no other reason. The opening of the great Southwest just at this time to land speculation, the production of a great staple like cotton, the immigration of planters all had the effect of diverting their attention for a

---

[24] Tucker, *United States*, 108–118; Meade, *Old Churches*, I., 90, note.

time, if not of raising a hope in anti-slavery men at the old South that the demand for slaves and the shifting of slave population might relieve the dangerous congestion of the black element and give time for devising a practicable means of realizing their aims; but these aims were not forgotten.[25] The exaggerated influence ascribed at the North in that day, and even in this, to cotton as the chief cause of the preservation of slavery is well refuted by the Rev. Dr. Nehemiah Adams of Boston, who early in the fifties spent three months in Georgia, South Carolina, and Virginia impartially studying the question of slavery. He was one of the New England clergy who framed a remonstrance against the extension of slavery into Nebraska and Kansas, and whose last act on leaving Boston was to sign this remonstrance. Regardless of preconceived opinions and anti-slavery sentiment, far more than Olmstead, the New York farmer, he was converted to the southern view of the question when he came into actual contact with the institution as practiced. He wrote a book for the benefit of his northern friends, which went through two editions, one in 1854 the other in 1860, whose motto was, " Hands off! The question is a domestic one best settled by the South and only delayed and hampered by interference from without." He explains the inactivity of southern anti-slavery men after 1832, not by cotton and reconversion to " avarice " and " immortality," but solely by the action of abolition societies at the North in scattering publications, as he says, " through the South, whose direct tendency was to stir up insurrection among the colored people. A travelling agent of a Northern society was arrested, and on searching his trunk there were found some prints which might well have wrought as they did upon the feelings of the Southern people. These prints were pictorial illustrations of the natural equality before God of all men without distinction of color, and setting forth the happy fruits of a universal acknowledgment of this

---

[25] Dew, *Debate*, 113.

truth, by exhibiting a white woman in no equivocal relations to a colored man.   Incendiary sentiments and pictures had for some time made their appearance on Northern handkerchiefs for Southern children and servants.   The old-fashioned blue-paper wrappers of chocolate had within them some eminently suggestive emblems.   When these amalgamation pictures were discovered, husbands and fathers at the South considered that whatever might be true of slavery as a system, self-defense, the protection of their households against a servile insurrection, was their first duty.   Who can wonder that they broke into the post-office and seized and burned abolition papers ; indeed no excesses are surprising in view of the perils to which they saw themselves exposed.   Then ensued those more stringent laws, so general now throughout the slave-holding States forbidding the slave to be publicly instructed.   Those laws remain to this present day ; they are disregarded indeed to a very great extent by the people themselves, but they remain in order to be enforced against Northern interference.   To the question why various things are not done to improve the condition of the blacks, the perpetual answer from men and women, who seek no apology is ' we are afraid of your abolitionists.' Whoever moves for redress in any of these things is warned that he is playing into the hands of Northern fanatics.   They seem to be living in a state of self-defense, of self-preservation against the North—as Northern zeal has promulgated bolder sentiments with regard to the right and duty of slaves to steal, burn, and kill in effecting their liberty, the South has intrenched itself by more vigorous laws and customs.   Nothing forces itself more constantly upon the thoughts of a Northerner at the South, who looks into the history and present state of slavery, than the vast injury which has resulted from Northern interferences." [26]

The best energy of both sections was wasted on slavery polemics on one side and apologetics on the other.   To accuse

---

[26] Adams, *South-Side View of Slavery*, 7, 11; 106, 107, 108, 110.

the slave-holder of sin *per se* demanded a moral and ethical defense, and volume after volume appeared against the doctrines of anti-slavery tract societies, either shifting a like responsibility for the sin upon the accuser's shoulders or asserting Divine as well as historic sanction for the institution. Little calm consideration could be given in this war of words and prejudice to the true economic' and political relations and effects of the institution, but a few of the apologists, like Dabney, Fitzhugh, and Smith made certain contributions toward an attempted scientific defense of the Virginia system, negativing some unhistorical *a priori* conceptions and deductions of Jefferson and his followers. Dabney and Fitzhugh showed conclusively that the social and economic fault lay not wholly with the system of slavery, but with the inevitable black population which Virginia had earnestly tried to exclude and failed, and with exclusive agriculture and non-rotating crops after the period of natural exploitation was over. Simple emancipation was merely postponement, not solution of the problem, and raised more grievous issues than slavery itself. Smith, in his lectures to college students and the public, applied his logic to refute the Jeffersonian doctrine of rights and the arguments for immediate, simultaneous, and progressive emancipation. The first and second propositions were politically and economically impossible. The third would entirely shift the burden upon the slave States to the South, as had been done by the action of laws in the northern States, that emancipated not slaves, but the after born, and few of these it was claimed. Admitting the proposed progression, first the District of Columbia, Delaware, and Maryland, then Virginia, then Kentucky, then Missouri, etc., as a cordon of buffer States would be relieved. The result would be to congest slaves by hundreds and thousands in the hands of a few proprietors in the Southwest, which would eliminate wholly the domestic element—the chief mitigating influence of slavery—and render the slave a mere instrument of toil, an economic machine in the hands not of the absentee employer but of his steward or agent, a result which could only be termed "brutal." [27]

The effect of constant attack and repulse in periodical literature, books and, last but not least, in the daily press was that the question of emancipation in Virginia was wholly obliterated in the irritated state of general public sentiment which was already wrought to such a pitch of excitement by other public questions, that the only arbitrament for one and all was in recourse to arms. Several acts of legislation nevertheless favored freedom in this troublous period, such as the provision of the code of 1849, interpreted by the courts to free the increase of any female slave, though born before her manumission went into effect. This was repeated in the code of 1860. But the strength of the reaction is shown not only in the disqualifying legislation against slaves and free negroes, but in a law of 1855–56 which opened a way for enslaving free negroes by allowing their re-creation as slaves by free acknowledgment upon their petitions in a court of record, like an English villain. They were carefully guarded by formal procedure against injustice and undue persuasion, however, in this. Another instance was the decision by the Court of Appeals, contrary to accepted legal opinion, against the general practice of allowing a slave, given the option of liberty by will, to make the choice or to contract for his liberty. Finally a law, passed at the called session of 1862, to protect and indemnify citizens of Virginia, provided that if any judge, commissioner, or other officer or agent of the United States by a decree or judgment emancipated the slaves of any citizen of Virginia, he was liable for twice the slave's value. Yet it has been estimated that Virginians, "without any legal compulsion" and by "private beneficence," freed at least 100,000 blacks, as against a total of 59,421 freed in the entire North by legal means. The last act in the drama of emancipation can scarcely be called the act of the representa-

---

[27] Smith, *Philosophy and Practice of Slavery*, 210-218, *et seq.*

tives of Virginia, but that of the agents of the General Government ratifying its will at the close of civil strife.

The status of the free negro had been of that gradual definition for cause, in law and custom, that we have seen marked that of various dependents. It had been a shifting though developing status of personal and political liberty, but not yet of full social freedom. The law required that a certificate of freedom, numbered and registered, should be given the freedman to protect him in his liberty. Without this proof he still had recourse to two modes of suit to establish freedom against his former master, (1) in law, *in forma pauperis* as prescribed by statute, (2) in equity when there was an impediment at law. In legacies it was done by propounding the will for probate. Against third parties claiming him as a slave he could proceed by writ of *habeas corpus,* and the jury might allow damages pending suit. The disabilities of his status were partly the result of the abuse of his liberty and his frequent connection with rebellion. By the restrictive slave law of 1723 freedmen were still allowed to enlist as musicians and laborers in the militia, and if housekeepers or frontiersmen, might keep ammunition and arms. In 1797 license was necessary for peddling and trading, to protect the property of whites, and for many offenses the freedman suffered not only the same penalty as whites but 39 lashes in addition. The immigration of the freed element was also restricted. As a defaulting tax-payer in 1819 the free negro could be hired out at a minimum rate until the levy was paid,[28] as a vagrant or illicit trader with slaves he could be enslaved for five years, and it was a duty of the overseers of the poor to make quarterly inspections into the condition of the freedmen. Between 1823 and 1828, for crimes punishable with confinement in the penitentiary for two years, and for the offense of beating or assaulting a white with intent to kill, free negroes were punish-

---

[28] Acts, 1822-3-25, 234, 238; 1831, April 7; 1832, March 15; Leigh, *Reports,* II., 652; Const. 1864, Art. IV., Grattan, *Reports,* XXII., 466.

able at the discretion of the court or jury with stripes or transportation as slaves.   The penalty was then made from five to
ten years in the penitentiary for the first offense and life imprisonment for the second.   Until 1825 petit larceny and
grand larceny were punishable only by stripes, but grand
larceny thereafter to the value of $10 involved whipping
and transportation.   The laws in the thirties became much
harsher, owing to the abolition movement and the fear of
insurrection.   The act of 1831 prohibiting assemblies or hired
teachers for slaves included free negroes, as also did that of
1832 against preaching.   Besides this the privilege of carrying arms was taken away, and a prohibition laid on selling or
giving away of liquor within a mile of any assembly of whites
or blacks.   Negroes paid the death penalty for assaults with
intent to kill, or upon a second offense of inciting rebellion,
and they were to be tried as slaves except in cases of homicide
and capital crime.   For receiving goods from slaves they were
punished by fine and imprisonment not exceeding $50 and six
months, and for selling liquor to slaves they were fined from
$10 to $50.   To ravish a white woman, maid or child was a
capital crime.   A free negro could hold slaves only by descent,
not by purchase, " other than husband, wife, parent or descendant."   But a will leaving him all the testator's estate, com-
prising slaves, was valid and the slaves would be sold for his
benefit.   In 1843 he was allowed to trade upon the certificate
of a respectable white person that he came by his goods
honestly..   In 1853 the city of Richmond passed an ordinance
prohibiting free negroes from keeping cook shops.   The free
negroes' chief civil incapacities were prohibition from the
suffrage after 1723, from office holding and from giving testimony against whites.[29]

The relation of the negro to crime and disorder, as most
of these disabilities show, caused great restrictions and the

---

[29] Leigh, *Reports*, IV., 649; Grattan, *Reports*, XII., 17; XIV.; Acts, 1831,
20; Code, 1849, 458; 1858, 46; 1843, 59; Code, 1860, 520, note.

numerous provisions for their transportation, taxation, and non-importation. After the Nat Turner insurrection the people of Northampton County took steps to raise $15,000 for the transportation of free negroes, and their action was legally sanctioned. The penitentiary reports up to 1829 showed that the proportion of convictions was one for every 16,000 whites, 1 for every 22,000 slaves, and 1 for every 5,000 free negroes.[30] The census reports from 1840 to 1860 indicated a very great moral and physical deterioration on the part of the free blacks as compared with the slaves and whites.

At the close of the civil war emigration at once began from country districts to towns, and cities, producing there a floating element of unoccupied, or at best but partially occupied, persons, and left in the agricultural regions, a dearth of their efficient labor skilled by long usage. Dabney states that almost immediately after emancipation, "grists" fell off by half, showing the negro's small food production and consumption, and their personal equipment was soon reduced by nearly two-thirds.[31] The general economic depression of the State naturally fell hardest upon the lowly landless freedman, and his rise has been of necessity slower and conditioned upon the gradual improvement of the welfare of the class which alone gives him an employment. His economic as his political future is thus inseparably bound up with that of his former master, with whose true interests his own are identical.

---

[30] Dew, *Debate*, 40, 95.
[31] Dabney, *Virginia*, 90, 92, note.

# BIBLIOGRAPHY.

MANUSCRIPT.

Accomac County Court Records (1632–). State Library, Richmond, Virginia.

Byrd, William, Sr., Letter Book of (1683–1691). Virginia Historical Society, Richmond, Virginia.

Collingwood, Edward. MSS. 2 v., folio. Library of Congress, Washington, D. C.

De Jarnette. MSS. 2 v., folio. State Library, Richmond, Virginia.

Essex County Court Records (1683–86). State Library, Richmond, Virginia.

Fitzhugh, William. Letter Book of (1679–1699). Virginia Historical Society.

General Court of Virginia, Records of (1670–1676). Virginia Historical Society.

Henrico County Court Records (1686–99). State Library, Richmond, Virginia.

Jefferson, Thomas. MSS. of (1606–1711). 7 v., folio. Letters, Patents, Proclamations, Orders and Instructions to Governors, Council Book (1679–1700), Laws (1623–1711). Library of Congress, Washington.

Land Books (1621–). Land Office, State Capitol, Richmond, Virginia.

MacDonald, Col. Angus M. MSS. relating to the early history of Virginia. 7 v., folio. State Library, Richmond, Virginia.

Randolph, John, of Roanoke. MSS. 3 v., folio. Virginia Historical Society.

Robinson, Conway. MSS. Abstracts of General Court Records and other valuable papers since destroyed. Virginia Historical Society, Richmond, Virginia.

Rockbridge County, Order Book of the Court. Folio. Lexington, Virginia.

Virginia MSS. from the British Public Record Office, Sainsbury and Winder collections, &c. 20 v., folio. State Library, Richmond, Virginia.

York County Court Records (1633–1709). State Library, Richmond, Virginia.

PUBLISHED.

Adams, Nehemiah. A South Side View of Slavery. 8vo. Boston, 1854.

Anburey, T. Travels through America. 2 vols., 8vo. London, 1789.

Anson, Sir William R.   The Principles of the English Law of Contract. 3rd ed.  Oxford, 1884.

Ashley, W. J.   Introduction to English Economic History and Theory. 2nd ed.  12mo.  London, 1893.

Arkansas Laws.  1843.

Ballagh, J. C.   White Servitude in the Colony of Virginia.  Johns Hopkins University Studies.  Baltimore, 1895.

Baltimore Sun.  1899.

Bancroft, George.   History of the United States of America.  6 v., 8vo. New York, 1883.

Bassett, John S.   History of Slavery in North Carolina.  J. H. U. Studies.  Baltimore, 1899.

Beverley, Robert.   History of Virginia.  Reprint from the 2nd London ed.  Richmond, 1855.

Belissario and Hetherington.   Trial of Arthur Hodge, Esq.

Blackstone, Sir Wm.   Commentaries on the Laws of England.  4 v. New York, 1859.

Blair, Chilton and Hartwell.  Present State of Virginia.  London, 1727.

Brackett, J. R.   The Negro in Maryland.  J. H. U. Studies.  Extra volume VI.  Baltimore, 1889.

Brown, Alexander.   The Genesis of the United States.  2 v.  Boston, 1890.

Bruce, John.   Annals of the Honorable East India Company.  3 v., 4to.  London, 1810.

Bruce, Philip A.   Economic History of Virginia in the Seventeenth Century.  2 v.  New York, 1896.

Burk, John Daly.  History of Virginia.  4 v., 8vo.  Petersburg, 1804–16.

Burke, Edmund.   European Settlements in America.  2nd ed.  2 v., 8vo.  London, 1785.

Byrd, Col. William.   History of the Dividing Line and other Tracts (Westover MSS., vol. II).  Richmond, 1866.

Cairnes, J. E.   The Slave Power, its Character, Career and Probable Designs.  2nd ed.  8vo.  London, 1863.

Calendar of English State Papers.  Colonial series.  1513–1676.  6 v., 8vo.  Ed. by W. Noel Sainsbury, London, 1860, 1862, 1880. Domestic Series, 27 v. Ed. by Mary A. Green.  17 v. Ed. by J. Bruce and W. D. Hamilton.

Calendar of Virginia State Papers and other MSS., preserved in the Capitol at Richmond, Ed. by Wm. P. Palmer.  6 v., 4to.  Richmond, 1875–86.

Campbell, Charles.   History of the Colony and Dominion of Virginia. Philadelphia, 1860.

Campbell, Rev. Dr. R. F.   The Race Problem in the South.  Pamphlet. 1899.

Census of the United States.  Decennial, 1790–1860.  Washington, D. C.

Chalmers, George. Political Annals of the Present United Colonies. 4 v. London, 1780.

Chase, H. and Sanborn, C. W. The North and the South. Boston, 1856.

Chastellux, F. J. Travels in North America. 2 v., 8vo. London, 1787.

Cobb, T. R. R. Law of Negro Slavery in the Various States of the United States. 8vo. Philadelphia, 1856.

Cooke, John Esten. Virginia, a History of the People. Boston, 1884.

Cooley, H. S. Slavery in New Jersey. J. H. U. Studies. Baltimore, 1897.

Cunningham, Wm. Growth of English Industry and Commerce in Modern Times. 8vo. Cambridge, 1892.

Curry, Dr. J. L. M. The Southern States of the American Union, &c. 8vo. Richmond, 1895.

Dabney, Rev. Dr. R. L. Defense of Virginia, and through Her of the South. 16mo. New York, 1867.

DeBow, J. B. D. Industrial Resources of the Southern and Western States. 3 v., 8vo. New Orleans, 1852, 1853.

Dew, Thomas. Review of the Debate in the Virginia Assembly of 1831-32. Madison Pamphlets, vol. 14.

Doyle, J. A. The English Colonies in America. 3 v. New York, 1882.

Drewry, W. S. The Southampton Insurrection. Washington, 1900.

Eddis, Wm. Letters from America, historical and descriptive. 1769-1777. 8vo. London, 1792.

Edwards, Bryan. History, Civil and Commercial of the British Colonies in the West Indies. 3 v., 8vo. 4th ed. London, 1807.

Elliot, J. Debates on the Federal Constitution. 5 v. Washington, 1836.

Fitzhugh, G. Sociology for the South. Richmond, 1854.
—— Cannibals All, or Slaves without Masters. Richmond, 1857.

Fitzhugh, Wm. Letters of. Virginia Magazine of History and Biography.

Fontaine, Rev. J. Memoirs of a Huguenot Family. New York, 1872.

Force, Peter. Tracts and other Papers relating to the Colonies in North America. 4 v., 8vo. Washington, 1836-46.

Franklin, Benjamin. Works of. Ed. by B. J. Bigelow. 10 v. New York, 1887.

Hamor, Ralph. True Discourse. 1614.

Hakluyt, Richard. Collection of Early Voyages, Travels and Discoveries of the English Nation. 5 v., 4to. London, 1809-12.

Helps, Sir Arthur. Spanish Conquest in America. 3 v. London, 1856.

Hening, Wm. Waller. Statutes at Large of Virginia. 13 v., 8vo. Richmond, 1812.

—— The New Virginia Justice. Richmond, 1799.

Henry, William Wirt. Life of Patrick Henry. New York, 1891.

Herrera, Histoire Generale des Voyages et Conquetes des Castillans. 4to. Paris, 1771.

Hildreth, R. History of the United States. 6 v. New York, 1856.

Howe, Henry. Historical Collections of Virginia. Charleston, 1852.

Howison, R. R. History of Virginia. 2 v., 8vo. Philadelphia, 1846–48.

—— History of the United States of America. Richmond, 1892.

Hotten, J. C. Original Lists of Emigrants. 1600–1700. London, 1874.

Hundley, D. R. Social Relations in our Southern States. 8vo. New York, 1860.

Hurd, John C., LL. D. The Law of Freedom and Bondage in the United States. 2 v., 8vo. Boston, 1858–62.

Illinois, Session Acts of. 1827.

Jefferson, Thomas. Writings of. Ed. by H. A. Washington. 9 v., 8vo. New York, 1859; Writings of. Ed. by P. L. Ford. 4 v. New York, 1892; Notes on Virginia. 8vo. London, 1787; Reports of Cases, General Court of Virginia. 1730–1740 and 1768–1792. 8vo. Charlottesville, 1829.

Justinian. Institutes of, with an introduction by Moyle, J. B. Oxford, 1883.

Jones, Rev. Hugh. Present State of Virginia. 8vo. New York, 1865.

Kalm, Peter. Travels into North America. 3 v., 8vo. London, 1771.

Kentucky, Revised Statutes of. 1852.

Lecky, W. E. H. History of England in the Eighteenth Century. 4 v., 8vo. London, 1878–82.

Lefroy, Sir John Henry. Memorials of the Bermudas, or Somers Islands. 2 v., 8vo. London, 1877–79.

Lexington, Virginia, Gazette. 1879.

Lodge, Henry Cabot. A Short History of the English Colonies. Rev. ed. New York, 1881.

McCrady, Edward. Slavery in the Province of South Carolina. Amer. Hist. Assoc. Reports, 1895. Washington, D. C.

McPherson, J. H. T. A History of Liberia. J. H. U. Studies in History and Politics. Baltimore, 1891.

Madison, James. Papers of. Ed. by H. D. Gilpin. 3 v., 8vo. New York, 1844.

Massachusetts Historical Society Collections. 4th ser. 6 v., 8vo. Boston, 1852–65.

Massachusetts, Statutes of. 1705, 1782.

Meade, Bishop W. Old Churches and Families of Virginia. 2 v. Philadelphia, 1878–85.

Middlesex County, England, Records. 4 v. Ed. by Jeaffreson, J. C. 1888.

Minor, John B., LL. D. Institutes of Common and Statute Law. 4 v. Richmond.

Moore, G. W. History of Slavery in Massachusetts. 8vo. New York, 1866.

Neill, E. D. History of the Virginia Company of London (1606-1624). 4to. Albany, 1869; Virginia Carolorum (1625-1685). Albany, 1869; The English Colonization of America. London, 1871; Virginia Vetusta. 1885.

North Carolina, Laws. 1723; Revised Statutes of. 1826.

Oldmixon, John. British Empire in America. 2 v., 12mo. London, 1708.

Olmstead, F. L. Our Slave States. London, 1856.

—— Journey in the Back Country. 8vo. London, 1861.

Pennsylvania, Acts of the General Assembly. 1700-1797. 4 v.

Plymouth Colonial Records.

Purchas, Samuel. Pilgrimes. 5 v., folio. London, 1625-26.

Rabbeno, Ugo. The American Commercial Policy. 8vo. London, 1895.

Randolph, T. J. Memoirs of Jefferson. 2 v. 1829.

Reeves, J. History of the English Law. Finlason edition. 5 v. 1880.

Richmond, Standard. 1800; Examiner. 1800; Virginian. 1808; Whig. 1831-32; Enquirer. 1831 and 1840. Richmond, Virginia.

Royal Commission on Historical Manuscripts, Reports of the. 8 v. London, 1870-81.

Smith, Capt. John. General History. 2 v., 8vo. Richmond, 1819.

—— Works (1608-1631). Ed. by Arber. 8vo. Birmingham, 1884.

Smith, W. A. The Philosophy and Practice of Slavery. Nashville, 1856.

Snelgrave, Capt. Wm. New Account of Guinea, &c. 8vo. London, 1734.

Sohm, R. The Institutes of Roman Law. Oxford, 1892.

Spotswood, Gov. Alexander. Official Letters of. 2 v. Va. Hist. Coll. Ed. by Brock, R. A. Richmond, 1882.

Statutes at Large of England and Great Britain. 20 v. London, 1811.

Steiner, Bernard S. Slavery in Connecticut. J. H. U. Studies. Baltimore, 1893.

Statutes at Large of Virginia, and Acts of Assembly. 1792-1866.

Stith, Wm. History of the Discovery and Settlement of Virginia. New York, 1865.

Strachey, W. Historie of Travaile into Virginia Britannia. Ed. by Major, R. H. Hakluyt Society, v. 6, 1849.

—— Lawes Divine, Morall and Martial. 1612. Force, v. 3.

Stroude, G. M. A Sketch of the Laws relating to Slavery in the several States of the United States of America. 8vo. Philadelphia, 1827.

Surtees Society, Publications of the. 84 v., 8vo. London, 1835-89.

Thurloe, John. Collections of State Papers. Ed. by Birch, T. 7 v. London, 1742.

Tucker, St. George. Commentaries on Blackstone. 2 v. Richmond.
—— Slavery in Virginia. Pamphlet.

Tucker, George. Progress of the United States. 8vo. New York, 1853.

Vance, W. R. Slavery in Kentucky. Pamphlet, 1896.

Vinogradoff, P. Villainage in England. Oxford, 1892.

Virginia Cases, 5 v. 1789-51.

Virginia, Colonial Records of. 1619-1680. State Senate Document. 4to.
—— Constitutions of. 1851, 1864, 1878.
—— Codes of. 1814, Revised. 1819, 1849, 1860.
—— Declaration of the State of the Colony of. London, 1620.
—— Gazettes. 1737-, Virginia Historical Society, Richmond.
—— Historical Register. Ed. by Maxwell, Wm. 6 v. Richmond, 1848.
—— New Description of. 1649. (Force, II.)
—— Historical Magazine. 8 v. 1-6 Ed. by P. A. Bruce. V. 6-8 Ed. by W. G. Stanard. Richmond.
—— Historical Society. Collections of. 10 v. Ed. by R. A. Brock. Richmond, 1882-91.
—— Reports of Cases determined in the General Court and in Court of Appeals of. (Jefferson, Washington, Call, Hening and Munford, Munford, Gilmer, Randolph, Leigh, Robinson, Grattan), 57 v. 1730-1865. Charlottesville, Philadelphia and Richmond.

Washington, George. Writings of. Ed. by W. C. Ford. 9 v. N. Y., 1889.
—— *Ibid.* Ed. by Jared Sparks. 12 v. Boston.

Whittaker, Alexander. Good Newes from Virginia. London, 1613.

Williams, E. Virginia Truly Valued. London, 1650.

Williams, G. W. History of the Negro Race in America. New York, 1883.

Wirt, William. Life of Patrick Henry. Philadelphia, 1817.

# INDEX.

## A.

Abolition of slavery, sentiment for, 127, 130.
Abolitionists, 131, 137, 138, 141–3.
Acts, mode of publication of, 78, 79.
Adams, *Rev. Dr.* Nehemiah, on slavery, 141, 142.
Africa, 3, 17 note, 21, 22.
African Company, 5, 10, 12, 13, 16, 17 note, 18.
African Colonization Society, 111, 136, 137.
Alabama, compared with Virginia in negro population, 25.
Alexander, *Rev. Dr.* Archibald, preaches to slaves, 110.
Alienation, incident of, 62, 65, 69.
Annexation, of slaves to land, 65–67.
Apprentices, English statute of, 41.
Apprenticeship, in Virginia, 45, 49 and note, 58.
Argall, Samuel, 7, 9 note.
Arkansas, law similar to Virginia, 61 and note.

## B.

Barbadoes, 6.
Barr, John, manumits slaves by will, 120.
Bermudas, negroes in the, 6–9; dependence in the, 29 and note, 30.
Bowles, Jack, in Gabriel's plot, 92.
Brass, case of the negro servant, 30, 31 and note.
Bristol, England, slave traders oppose duties, 16.
Brown, Alexander, 8 note.
Bruce, Philip Alexander, 8 note.
Blacks, 3, 12, 24, 134; in proportion to whites in Massachusetts, 134; overdensity of, in Virginia, 139, 141, 143; freed by Virginia, 144.

## C.

Carolinas, slaves in the, 6, 12, 13 note, 19, 21, 25.
Carthagena, expedition against, 20.
Census, Virginia, of 1623, 29 note.
Chavis, *Rev.* John, *colored*, 110.
Christian, legal use of the term, 47, 49.
Christianity, its effects as to liberty, 46, 48, 51 note, 52.
Churches, negro, 111, 114; negroes in white, 113.
Clergy, Benefit of, 78, 85, 86.
*Clientela*, institution of, 2.
Code, slave, diminished rigor of, 83, 84.
Colonies, English, 4–6, 12, 19; Spanish, 5, 6, 12.
Colonization of negroes, proposed, 132, 133, 136, 138; criticised by Tucker, 134; emigration as a substitute for, 135; legislative appropriations for, 136, 137.
Color line, discriminations of the, 56, 57, 62.
*Comitatus*, 2.
Commerce, Spanish, 7; policy of English, 14, 19, 21.
Commutation, principle of, 86, 87, 118, 119.
Company, see African; South Sea, 5; Summers Island, 6; Virginia, 7.
Connecticut, slavery in, 34, 36, 37 note.
Contracts, with servants, 40, 42, 43; with Indians, 49; with slaves, 72, 73, 107.
Convicts, imported, 23.
Court, General, of Virginia decisions, 31 note, 33, 50 and note, 64, 75, 76, 82; procedure in trials of slaves, 82–84; ruling of Massachusetts General, on slavery, 36; of

Appeals decisions, 51, 54, 63, 81;
Richmond hustings, 84; jurisdiction of a corporation, as to slaves,
84.
Crime, increase of, 82, capital, 73
and note, 85, 86, 146.
Criminal procedure, as to slaves, 83;
as to free men, 84, 85.
Crown, policy as to duties on slaves,
17-20; petitions to the, 20, 22.

### D.

Dabney, *Rev. Dr.* R. L., on slavery,
101.
Davis, Hugh, pnnished, 57.
Deportation of negroes, proposed,
138.
Dew, Thomas, 101; report of debate
on slave emancipation, 137-138.
Dinwiddie, *Governor,* of Virginia, 68.
Dismemberment, as a punishment,
84.
*Dominium,* right of, 2, 31.
Dower, in slaves, 63, 124.
Drewry, W. S., his work on the
Southampton Insurrection, 94 note.
Duquesne, fall of Fort, 21.
Dutch, privateers, 28; importation
of negroes by the, 35 note.
Duties, import, on slaves, 11, 15 and
note, 16-21.
Drawbacks, for exportation of slaves,
19.

### E.

Education, of dependents, 109, 111,
113.
Elizabeth, Queen, interested in the
slave trade, 5.
Emancipation, in Roman law, 116;
realization of, in Europe, 118;
relation of freedmen to, 126, 127;
sentiment for, 127, 128, 130; plans
for general, 24, 130-139; estimated cost of, 131, 133, 138;
causes for failure of proposals for,
136, 139; progressive, 143; reaction against, 144.
Emigration, of whites from Virginia,
139; of negroes from country districts, 147.

England, 4, 7, 11, 13-16, 17, 20, 22,
recognizes slavery, 34; condition
of labor in, 40, 41.
Entails, 65-67; abolished, 68.
Equality, doctrine of natural, 2, 129;
affirmed by the Virginia Declara-
tion of Rights, 53 and note.
Estates, legal, in slaves, 64-68.
Europe, slave trade in, 4.
Evidence, of colored persons received,
73, 83.
Extradition, of slaves, 76.

### F.

Fitzhugh, George, on slavery, 143.
Fontaine, *Col.* Peter, 17, 21 note, 59.
Forfeiture, of slaves, 65.
Freedmen, see Free negroes.
Freedom, provisions of the Code in
favor of, 144; purchase of, 107,
108, 111; free services an evidence
of, 119; favorable attitude of
courts toward, 123, 124; by statute,
123; simple procedure in suits for,
71, 73, 123, 145; certificates of,
124, 145.
Free negroes, importation of, 24;
emigration of, 26; rights of, 71,
72, 73; menace of, 56, 119; enslavement of, 56, 144; discriminations against, 62, 119, 145; number of, 121; sentiment for removal
of, 126, 136, 137, 147; status of,
97, 145, 146; as slave-holders, 146;
and crime, 147.

### G.

Gabriel, plot of the slave, 92.
Georgia, compared with Virginia as
to negro population, 25.
Gonzales, Antony, 3.

### H.

Harper, Robert Goodloe, aids African colonization, 136.
Hawkins, *Sir* John, as a slave
trader, 4.
Head rights, 10.

Henry, Prince, of Portugal, 3.
Henry, Patrick, on slavery, 130.
Heredity, principle of, in slavery, 38.
Hill, *Rev. Dr.* Wm., 110.
Hodge, Arthur, of Virgin Islands, hung, 82.
Holidays, slave, 74, 108.
Huston, John, case of, 81.

## I.

Incidents of servitude pass to slavery, 32, 37, 40, 62; effect of modification of, 39; legal origin of, 43; as result of the property conception, 62, 63; resulting from rebellion, 95.
Independence, Declaration of, 22, 23, 53.
Indentured servitude, 41.
Indians, 6, 7, 14, 20, 72, 74, 79; enslavement of, 35, 36, 48, 50, 51; danger from, 38, 44, 89, 119; protected from enslavement, 47, 49, 50; slave trade by, 48; acts concerning, 49, 50 and note.
Insurrection, plots of, 11, 78, 79; an anticipated danger, 89; fear of, affects legislation, 91, 92; in Southampton County, 93.

## J.

Jackson, *Gen.* T. J., teaches negroes, 113.
Jamestown, first negroes at, 8,
Jasper, *Rev.* John, colored preacher, 94 note.
Jefferson, Thomas, on slavery, 16, 24, 128–130; his bill abolishing entails, 68; plans emancipation, 131–133.
Jews, as slaves, 46, 53; disability of free, 58.
Justinian, on sources of slavery, 44.

## K.

Kentucky, legislation affected by Virginia, 61 and note.

## L.

Labor, dependent, 2, 4, 6; scarcity of, 10; free-contract, develops into servitude, 32; relation of negroes to, 109, 110; proportion of slaves to whites in agricultural, 134.
Lagos, Company of, 3.
Land values, supposed to depend on slavery, 138.
Las Casas, Bishop, his relation to negro slavery, 4, 46.
Lease system, as to slaves, 106.
Legislation, explanation of restrictive, 89.
Liberia, colony of, 136, 137.
Liquor, duties on, 14.
Liverpool, slave traders of, 16.

## M.

Madison, James, opposes slavery, 130.
Manumission, in Roman law, 116; in English law, 117; restrictions on, 119, 120, 125, 126; modes of, 120–122; records of, 124; number benefitting by, 144.
Maine, *Sir* Henry, on contractural brigin of slavery, 42.
Marriages, mixed, 9; discouraged, 57; prohibited, 75; of whites and Indians, 59.
Maryland, 12, 13 note, 21, 25, 26, 33; African Colonization Society of, 136.
Massachusetts, servitude and slavery in, 6, 33; Fundamentals, 34; papers accuse *Gov.* Seward, 76.
Masters, duties of, 75, 80, 95, 96, 98, 100; rights of, 37–39, 62, 76–78, 80; of vessels, 77; affection of slaves for, 98, 99, 106.
Master and servant, tie of, 99, 106.
Meade, *Rt. Rev.* William, on slavery, 140.
Mestizos, class of, 61.
Militia, exemptions from service in the, 73, 79; enlistment in the, 74; protection, 90, 91 note.
Mohammedans, enslaved, 46; disability of free, 58.
Monroe, James, aids African colonization, 136.

Moors, as slaves, 3, 48, 52 ; disability of free, 58.

Muster of Virginia population in 1624–25, 29 note.

Mulattoes, enslaved, 39, 43, 52, 60 ; class of free, 43 note, 45 ; increase of, 44, 59 ; small class of, 61 ; disabilities of, 58 ; penalty for sale of, 60 and note ; definition of, 58, 60, 61 ; treatment of, in the North, 62.

## N.

Nar, negroes from the island of, 3.

Negroes, importation of, 3, 5–8 and note, 9–11, 14 ; prices of, 13 ; population of, 23, 24, 26 ; in the Bermudas and in Virginia not slaves, 8 and note, 28 ; servitude of, 29 note, 31, 32, 47 ; enslaved, 10, 34, 39, 46, 47, 52, 56 ; viewed as men, 54 ; discrimination against, 56, 88, 95 ; definition of, 59, 61 and note ; restrictions on marriage with, 57, 59, 62 ; as doctors, 86 ; education of, 109–111, 113 ; as church members, 111, 113.

New York, 76 ; civil law sanction of slavery in, 34.

North Carolina, encourages African colonization, 136.

Nicholson, Governor, discontinues land grants for imported slaves, 13.

## O.

Olmstead, F. W., on slavery, 141.

Overseers, 73, 75, 102–104.

## P.

*Patria potestas*, at Rome, 2, 80, 116.

Patrol, for slaves and servants, 89, 90 ; powers of the, 91.

Payne, James S., *colored*, President of Liberia, 137.

*Peculium*, 71, 109.

Penick, *Rt. Rev.* Charles C., missionary to Liberia, 137.

Penitentiary, 76.

Pharoah, warning of Gabriel's plot by the slave, 92.

Piracy, 7, 8, 16.

Plantations, 75, 76 ; extent and location of, 105.

Population, negro and white, 11, 12, 24, 25.

Portugal, commercial expansion of, 3, 4.

*Potestas, dominica*, at Rome, 40.

Preston, *Col.* J. T. L., 113.

Public works, revenue from slave importations expended on, 16 note.

## Q.

Quebec, fall of, 21.

## R.

Race, penalty for mixture of, 5, 7, 44 ; as criterion for slavery, 45, 56 ; extent of blood of, 58, 59.

Randolph, Thomas J., plans emancipation, 137, 138.

Rape, punishment of attempted, 84.

Rebellion, slave, 14, 91 ; penalty for advocating, 95.

Revenue, from slaves, 13, 14, 16, 18 ; royal, 17 ; acts, 15 note.

Revisals, of laws, 15 note, 56.

Revolution, the American, 5, 19, 23.

Rich, *Sir* Robert, 5, 7, 9 note.

Rights, doctrines of inalienable, 2, 129 ; Virginia Declaration of, 53.

Roman Law, on slavery, 38–40, 44.

## S.

Servants, 10, 15 note, 72, 73 ; negro and Indian, 35 ; sources of, 42 and note ; made slaves, 57 ; mulatto, 59, 60 ; convict and "spirited," 79 ; absconding, 80.

Servitude, institution of, 2, 31 note, 42, 72, 77 ; basis of slavery, 31, 32 ; product of customary law, 33 ; effect on slavery, 33 note ; legal sanction of, in the colonies, 36 ; transition into slavery, 37, 39 ;

colonial origin of, 41, 42; personel in, 42 note; as a legal penalty, 45.

Seward, *Gov.* William H., of New York, 76.

Slaves, legal status of, 9–96; social status of, 96–115; breeding of, 36, 98; rights of, 28, 71–75, 78, 95, 97, 102, 108, 109; legal designation of, 52, 53; vested interests in, 65; as personalty, 62, 63, 65, 69, 70; as realty, 63, 64, 66, 69, 70; entailed, 64; as currency, 69; liable to seizure, 62, 66, 67, 69; gifts of, 68; personalty of, 71–73, 82, 97; population of, 10, 134; taxation on, 11–21, 72; stealing of, 76, 77; killing of, 78, 81; when killing of, murder, 82; on trial defended by masters, 83; sueing for freedom privileged, 84; favored in criminal procedure, 85; reprieved for transportation, 86; favored in penal legislation, 88; commit few of the higher crimes, 89; restricted as to assemblies, 90; religious and secular instruction of, 90, 95, 109–114; family rights of, 97, 98, 102; in the family, 100, 118; maintenance of, 102–103; distribution of, 105; leases of, 76, 80, 106; occupations of, 107, 108; personal bond between masters and, 114; modes of establishing title to, 117; fugitive, 78, 125; when removed to other states, might be freed, 123, 124; exportation of female, 126; importation of, restricted, 125, 126; manumitted, 119–121, 123, 127, 144.

Slave dealers, greed of, 60.

Slave trade, European nations in the, 3–6; in the Bermudas and in Virginia, 6–23.

Slavery, African, 1–3; development of, 1, 27 *et seq.;* distinguishing mark of, 28; political and domestic, 29; statutory sanction of, 33, 34; of Indians, 35, 36, 47, 49, 51; customary sanction of, 36; doctrines of, 38, 57; statutory extension of, in the colonies, 39; natural sources of, 44; philosophic basis of, 45 *et seq.;* as a means of Christianization, 46; subjects of, 46, 48; nominal test of, 49; as a preventive

penalty, 51; incidents of, 65, 71–77; Roman, 71, 74; analogous to villainage, 96; patriarchal character of, 99, 100; tends toward servitude, 115, 118; its supposed effect on land values, 138; abolished, 145 and note; apologetics, 142–4.

Smith, *Rev. Dr.* John Blair, 110.

Smith, *Rev. Dr.* William A., lectures on slavery, 143.

Society, position of labor in industrial, 1, 2.

Southampton County, insurrection in, 93–5, 98.

Spain, in the slave trade, 4, 5.

Spotswood, *Gov.* Alexander, 14, 15, 16 and note.

Status, creation of legal, 27; imposed by English and Dutch on negroes, 28; of servitude changed to slavery, 37, 38; of dependent labor, 40; of the slave, 27–115; of freedom, a development, 117; transition of, 118.

Sugar, as a cause of importation to the Bermudas, 6.

Sunday Schools, for negroes, 133.

Sweet, Robert, punished, 57.


# T.

Tariff, see Duties.

Tax, incidence of that laid by duties on slaves, 17 and note; objection to a poll, 18.

Tobacco, low price of, 14, 15.

Trade, Lords of, 13; British, 17; Board of, 21 note.

Traders, English slave, 10, 12, 17 note, 18, 21; American slave, 21; views of, 48 note; domestic slave, 102, 105, 106.

*Treasurer,* the ship, 7 and note, 8, 9 and note.

Tucker, *Professor* George, on extinction of slavery, 139.

Tucker, St. George, on slave trials, 85; on racial discriminations, 89; on slavery, 129; plans emancipation, 24; 133–136.

Turks, as slaves, 48, 52.

Turner, Nat., negro preacher raises revolt, 93 *et seq.*

## U.

United States, agents emancipating slaves liable, 144; alleged violation of provision of the Constitution of, 76.
Utrecht, treaty of, affects the slave-trade, 5, 12.

## V.

Vassalage, European, 2, 28.
Villains, restrictions in the alienation of, 63; condition of, 66, 67; creation and enfranchisement of, 117.
Villainage, in England, 2, 28, 38-40, 65, 77, 117.
Vinogradoff, Paul, on the principle "regardant" in villainage, 66.
Virginia, efforts to restrict importation of slaves, 12-23; prohibits the slave-trade, 23; negro population in, 24-26; first negroes in, 28; servitude in, 33; sanction of slavery in, 34; Declaration of Rights of, 53, 55; Assembly of 1831-32, debates the question of emancipation, 99.

## W.

Washington, Bushrod, favors African colonization, 136.
Washington, George, on abolition of slavery, 130.
West Indies, Spanish, 3, 4, 6-8, 21; slave practice in Spanish, 98; French, 134.
White, *Rev. Dr.* William S., on the negro preacher " Jack," 112.
Whites, enslaved by Moors, 3; population of, 12, 24, 25, 134; race mixture of, with blacks. 44; banishment of, 45 note, 57, 58; discriminations in favor of, 57 and note, 78; discriminations against, 75.
Wythe, George, Chancellor of Virginia, advocates freedom, 54; as a codifier, 32.

## Z.

Zuñiga, Spanish Ambassador in England, on marriage of whites with Indians in Virginia, 59.

## ERRATA.

Page 8 note, *Immigrants* should be *Emigrants.*
Page 45, line 10 from bottom—the second "and" should be omitted.

JOHNS HOPKINS UNIVERSITY STUDIES

IN

# HISTORICAL AND POLITICAL SCIENCE.

(Edited by Herbert B. Adams, 1882–1901.)

## FIRST SERIES.—Local Institutions.—$4.00.

I. An Introduction to American Institutional History. By E. A. FREEMAN. 25 cents.
II. The Germanic Origin of New England Towns. By H. B. ADAMS. 50 cents.
III. Local Government in Illinois. By ALBERT SHAW.—Local Government in Pennsylvania. By E. R. L. GOULD. 30 cents.
IV. Saxon Tithingmen in America. By H. B. ADAMS. 50 cents.
V. Local Government in Michigan, and the Northwest. By E. W. BEMIS. 25 cents.
VI. Parish Institutions of Maryland. By EDWARD INGLE. 40 cents.
VII. Old Maryland Manors. By JOHN HEMSLEY JOHNSON. 30 cents.
VIII. Norman Constables in America. By H. B. ADAMS. 50 cents.
IX-X. Village Communities of Cape Ann and Salem. By H. B. ADAMS. 50 cents.
XI. The Genesis of a New England State. By A. JOHNSTON. 30 cents.
XII. Local Government and Schools in South Carolina. By B. J. RAMAGE. 40 cents.

## SECOND SERIES.—Institutions and Economics.—$4.00.

I-II. Methods of Historical Study. By H. B. ADAMS. 50 cents.
III. The Past and the Present of Political Economy. By R. T. ELY. 35 cents.
IV. Samuel Adams, The Man of the Town Meeting. By JAMES K. HOSMER. 35 cents.
V-VI. Taxation in the United States. By HENRY CARTER ADAMS. 50 cents.
VII. Institutional Beginnings in a Western State. By JESSE MACY. 25 cents.
VIII-IX. Indian Money in New England, etc. By WILLIAM B. WEEDEN. 50 cents.
X. Town and County Government in the Colonies. By E. CHANNING. 50 cents.
XI. Rudimentary Society among Boys. By J. HEMSLEY JOHNSON. 60 cents.
XII. Land Laws of Mining Districts. By C. H. SHINN. 50 cents.

## THIRD SERIES.—Maryland, Virginia and Washington.—$4.00.

I. Maryland's Influence upon Land Cessions to the U. S. By H. B. ADAMS. 75 cents.
II-III. Virginia Local Institutions. By E. INGLE. 75 cents.
IV. Recent American Socialism. By RICHARD T. ELY. 50 cents.
V-VI-VII. Maryland Local Institutions. By LEWIS W. WILHELM. $1.00.
VIII. The Influence of the Proprietors in Founding New Jersey. By AUSTIN SCOTT. 25 cents.
IX-X. American Constitutions. By HORACE DAVIS. 50 cents.
XI-XII. The City of Washington. By J. A. PORTER. 50 cents.

## FOURTH SERIES.—Municipal Government and Land Tenure.—$3.50.

I. Dutch Village Communities on the Hudson River. By I. ELTING. 50 cents.
II-III. Town Government in Rhode Island. By W. E. FOSTER.—The Narragansett Planters. By EDWARD CHANNING. 50 cents.
IV. Pennsylvania Boroughs. By WILLIAM P. HOLCOMB. 50 cents.
V. Introduction to Constitutional History of the States. By J. F. JAMESON. 50 cents.
VI. The Puritan Colony at Annapolis, Maryland. By D. R. RANDALL. 50 cents.
VII-VIII-IX. The Land Question in the United States. By S. SATO. $1.00.
X. Town and City Government of New Haven. By C. H. LEVERMORE. 50 cents.
XI-XII. Land System of the New England Colonies. By M. EGLESTON. 50 cents.

## FIFTH SERIES.—Municipal Government, History and Politics.—$3.50.

I-II. City Government of Philadelphia. By E. P. ALLINSON and B. PENROSE. 50 cents.
III. City Government of Boston. By JAMES M. BUGBEE. 25 cents.
IV. City Government of St. Louis. By MARSHALL S. SNOW. 25 cents.
V-VI. Local Government in Canada. By JOHN GEORGE BOURINOT. 50 cents.
VII. Effect of the War of 1812 upon the American Union. By NICHOLAS MURRAY BUTLER. 25 cents.
VIII. Notes on the Literature of Charities. By HERBERT B. ADAMS. 25 cents.
IX. Predictions of Hamilton and De Tocqueville. By JAMES BRYCE. 25 cents.
X. The Study of History in England and Scotland. By P. FRÉDÉRICQ. 25 cents.
XI. Seminary Libraries and University Extension. By H. B. ADAMS. 25 cents.
XII. European Schools of History and Politics. By A. D. WHITE. 25 cents.

**SIXTH SERIES.**—The History of Co-operation in the United States.—$3.50.

**SEVENTH SERIES.**—Social Science, Education, Government.—$3.50.

I. Arnold Toynbee. By F. C. MONTAGUE. 50 cents.
II-III. Municipal Government in San Francisco. By BERNARD MOSES. 50 cents.
IV. The City Government of New Orleans. By WM. W. HOWE. 25 cents.
V-VI. English Culture in Virginia. By WILLIAM P. TRENT. $1.00.
VII-VIII-IX. The River Towns of Connecticut. By CHARLES M. ANDREWS. $1.00.
X-XI-XII. Federal Government in Canada. By JOHN G. BOURINOT. $1.00.

**EIGHTH SERIES.**—History, Politics and Education.—$3.50.

I-II. The Beginnings of American Nationality. By A. W. SMALL. $1.00.
III. Local Government in Wisconsin. By D. E. SPENCER. 25 cents.
IV. Spanish Colonization in the Southwest. By F. W. BLACKMAR. 50 cents.
V-VI. The Study of History in Germany and France. By P. FRÉDÉRICQ. $1.00.
VII-IX. Progress of the Colored People of Maryland. By J. R. BRACKETT. $1.00.
X. The Study of History in Belgium and Holland. By P. FRÉDÉRICQ. 50 cents.
XI-XII. Seminary Notes on Recent Historical Literature. By H. B. ADAMS, J. M. VINCENT, W. B. SCAIFE, and others. 50 cents.

**NINTH SERIES.**—Education, History, Politics, Social Science.—$3.50.

I-II. Government and Administration of the United States. By W. W. WILLOUGHBY and W. F. WILLOUGHBY. 75 cents.
III-IV. University Education in Maryland. By B. C. STEINER. The Johns Hopkins University (1876-1891). By D. C. GILMAN. 50 cents.
V-VI. Development of Municipal Unity in the Lombard Communes. By WILLIAM K. WILLIAMS. 50 cents.
VII-VIII. Public Lands of the Roman Republic. By A. STEPHENSON. 75 cents.
IX. Constitutional Development of Japan. By T. IYENAGA. 50 cents.
X. A History of Liberia. By J. H. T. McPHERSON. 50 cents.
XI-XII. The Indian Trade in Wisconsin. By F. J. TURNER. 50 cents.

**TENTH SERIES.**—Church and State: Columbus and America.—$3.50.

I. The Bishop Hill Colony. By MICHAEL A. MIKKELSEN. 50 cents.
II-III. Church and State in New England. By PAUL E. LAUER. 50 cents.
IV. Church and State in Maryland. By GEORGE PETRIE. 50 cents.
V-VI. The Religious Development in the Province of North Carolina. By STEPHEN B. WEEKS. 50 cents.
VII. Maryland's Attitude in the Struggle for Canada. By J. W. BLACK. 50 cents.
VIII-IX. The Quakers in Pennsylvania. By A. C. APPLEGARTH. 75 cents.
X-XI. Columbus and his Discovery of America. By H. B. ADAMS and H. WOOD. 50 cents.
XII. Causes of the American Revolution. By J. A. WOODBURN. 50 cents.

**ELEVENTH SERIES.**—Labor, Slavery, and Self-Government.—$3.50.

I. The Social Condition of Labor. By E. R. L. GOULD. 50 cents.
II. The World's Representative Assemblies of To-Day. By E. K. ALDEN. 50 cents.
III-IV. The Negro in the District of Columbia. By EDWARD INGLE. $1.00.
V-VI. Church and State in North Carolina. By STEPHEN B. WEEKS. 50 cents.
VII-VIII. The Condition of the Western Farmer as illustrated by the economic history of a Nebraska township. By A. F. BENTLEY. $1.00.
IX-X. History of Slavery in Connecticut. By BERNARD C. STEINER. 75 cents.
XI-XII. Local Government in the South and Southwest. By EDWARD W. BEMIS and others. $1.00.

**TWELFTH SERIES.**—Institutional and Economic History.—$3.50.

I-II. The Cincinnati Southern Railway. By J. H. HOLLANDER. $1.00.
III. Constitutional Beginnings of North Carolina. By J. S. BASSETT. 50 cents.
IV. The Struggle of Protestant Dissenters for Religious Toleration in Virginia. By H. R. McILWAINE. 50 cents.
V-VI-VII. The Carolina Pirates and Colonial Commerce. By S. C. HUGHSON. $1.00.
VIII-IX. History of Representation and Suffrage in Massachusetts (1620-1691). By G. H. HAYNES. 50 cents.
X. English Institutions and the American Indian. By J. A. JAMES. 25 cents.
XI-XII. The International Beginnings of the Congo Free State. By J. S. REEVES. 50 cents.

**THIRTEENTH SERIES.**—South Carolina, Maryland, Virginia.—$3.50.

I-II. Government of the Colony of South Carolina. By E. L. WHITNEY. 75 cents.
III-IV. Early Relations of Maryland and Virginia. By J. H. LATANÉ. 50 cents.
V. The Rise of the Bicameral System in America. By T. F. MORAN. 50 cents.

VI-VII. White Servitude in the Colony of Virginia, By J. C. BALLAGH. 50 *cents*.
VIII. The Genesis of California's First Constitution. By R. D. HUNT. 50 *cents*.
IX. Benjamin Franklin as an Economist. By W. A. WETZEL. 50 *cents*.
X. The Provisional Government of Maryland. By J. A. SILVER. 50 *cents*,
XI-XII. Government and Religion of the Va. Indians. By S. R. HENDREN. 50 *cents*.

FOURTEENTH SERIES.—Baltimore, Slavery, Constitutional History.—$3.50.

I. Constitutional History of Hawaii. By HENRY E. CHAMBERS. 25 *cents*.
II. City Government of Baltimore. By THADDEUS P. THOMAS. 25 *cents*.
III. Colonial Origins of New England Senates. By F. L. RILEY. 50 *cents*.
IV-V. Servitude in the Colony of North Carolina. By J. S. BASSETT. 50 *cents*.
VI-VII. Representation in Virginia. By J. A. C. CHANDLER. 50 *cents*.
VIII. History of Taxation in Connecticut (1636-1776). By F. R. JONES. 50 *cents*.
IX-X. A Study of Slavery in New Jersey. By HENRY S. COOLEY. 50 *cents*.
XI-XII. Causes of the Maryland Revolution of 1689. By F. E. SPARKS. 50 *cents*.

FIFTEENTH SERIES.—American Economic History.—$3.50.

I-II. The Tobacco Industry in Virginia since 1860. By H. W. ARNOLD. 50 *cents*.
III-V. Street Railway System of Philadelphia. By F. W. SPEIRS. *Cloth*, $1.00.
VI. Daniel Raymond. By C. P. NEILL, 50 *cents*.
VII-VIII. Economic History of B. & O. R. R. By M. REIZENSTEIN. 50 *cents*.
IX. The South American Trade of Baltimore. By F. R. RUTTER. 50 *cents*.
X-XI. State Tax Commissions in the U. S. By J. W. CHAPMAN. 50 *cents*.
XII. Tendencies in American Economic Thought. By S. SHERWOOD. 25 *cents*.

SIXTEENTH SERIES.—Anglo-American Relations and Southern History.—$3.50.

I-IV. The Neutrality of the American Lakes, etc. By J. M. CALLAHAN. $1.50.
V. West Florida and its Relation to the Historical Carthography of the United States. By H. E. CHAMBERS. 25 *cents*.
VI. Anti-Slavery Leaders of North Carolina. By J. S. BASSETT. 50 *cents*.
VII-IX. Life and Administration of Sir Robert Eden. By B. C. STEINER. $1.00.
X-XI. The Transition of North Carolina from a Colony to a Commonwealth. By E. W. SIKES. 50 *cents*.
XII. Jared Sparks and Alexis De Tocqueville. By H. B. ADAMS. 25 *cents*.

SEVENTEENTH SERIES.—Economic History; Maryland and the South.—$3.50.

I-II-III. History of State Banking in Maryland. By A. C. BRYAN. $1.00.
IV-V. The Know-Nothing Party in Maryland. By L. F. SCHMECKEBIER. 75 *cents*.
VI. The Labadist Colony in Maryland. By B. B. JAMES. 50 *cents*.
VII-VIII. History of Slavery in North Carolina. By J. S. BASSETT. 75 *cents*.
IX-X-XI. Development of the Chesapeake & Ohio Canal. By G. W. WARD. 75 *cents*.
XII. Public Educational Work in Baltimore. By HERBERT B. ADAMS. 25 *cents*.

EIGHTEENTH SERIES.—Taxation in the Southern States: Church and Popular Education.—$3.50.

I-IV. Studies in State Taxation, with Particular Reference to the Southern States. Edited by J. H. HOLLANDER. Paper, $1.00; cloth, $1.25.
V-VI. The Colonial Executive Prior to the Restoration. By P. L. KAYE. 50 *cents*.
VII. Constitution and Admission of Iowa into the Union. By J. A. JAMES. 30 *cents*.
VIII-IX. The Church and Popular Education. By H. B. ADAMS. 50 *cents*.
X-XII. The Struggle for Religious Freedom in Virginia: The Baptists. By W. T. THOM. 75 *cents*.

NINETEENTH SERIES.—Diplomatic and Constitutional History.—$3.50.

I-III. America in the Pacific and the Far East. By J. M. CALLAHAN. 75 *cents*.
IV-V. State Activities in Relation to Labor in the United States. By W. F. WILLOUGHBY. 50 *cents*.
VI-VII. History of Suffrage in Virginia. By J. A. C. CHANDLER. 50 *cents*.
VIII-IX. The Maryland Constitution of 1864. By W. S. MYERS. 50 *cents*.
X. Life of Commissary James Blair, Founder of William and Mary College. By D. E. MOTLEY. 25 *cents*.
XI-XII. Gov. Hicks of Maryland and the Civil War. By G. L. RADCLIFFE. 50 *cents*.

The Johns Hopkins University Studies in Historical and Political Science appear monthly. The subscription is three dollars per year. Orders should be addressed to

THE JOHNS HOPKINS PRESS, BALTIMORE, MD.

# Extra Volumes of Studies

—— IN ——

# HISTORICAL AND POLITICAL SCIENCE.

**Philadelphia, 1681-1887.** By EDWARD P. ALLINSON, A. M., and BOIES PENROSE, A. B. 444 pages. 8vo. Cloth. $3.00.

**Baltimore and the Nineteenth of April, 1861.** By GEORGE WILLIAM BROWN, Chief Judge of the Supreme Bench of Baltimore, and Mayor of the City in 1861. 176 pages. 8vo. Cloth. $1.00.

**Local Constitutional History of the United States.** By GEORGE E. HOWARD, Ph. D. Volume I.—Development of the Township, Hundred and Shire. 542 pages. 8vo. Cloth. $3.00. Volume II.—In preparation.

**The Negro in Maryland.** By JEFFREY R. BRACKETT, Ph. D. 270 pages. 8vo. Cloth. $2.00.

**The Supreme Court of the United States.** By W. W. WILLOUGHBY, Ph. D. 124 pages. 8vo. Cloth. $1.25.

**The Intercourse between the U. S. and Japan.** By INAZO (OTA) NITOBE, Ph. D. 198 pages. 8vo. Cloth. $1.25.

**Spanish Institutions of the Southwest.** By FRANK W. BLACKMAR, Ph. D. 380 pages. 8vo. Cloth. $2.00.

**An Introduction to the Study of the Constitution.** By MORRIS M. COHN. 250 pages. 8vo. Cloth. $1.50.

**The Old English Manor.** By C. M. ANDREWS, Ph. D. 280 pages. 8vo. Cloth. $1.50.

**The Southern Quakers and Slavery.** By STEPHEN B. WEEKS, Ph. D. 414 pages. 8vo. Cloth. $2.00.

**Contemporary American Opinion of the French Revolution.** By C. D. HAZEN, Ph. D. 325 pages. 8vo. Cloth. $2.00.

**Industrial Experiments in the British Colonies of North America.** By ELEANOR L. LORD. 164 pages. 8vo. Cloth. $1.25.

**State Aid to Higher Education:** A Series of Addresses at the Johns Hopkins University. 100 pages. 8vo. Cloth. $1.00.

**Financial History of Baltimore.** By J. H. HOLLANDER, Ph. D. 400 pages. 8vo. Cloth. $2.00.

**Cuba and International Relations.** By J. M. CALLAHAN, Ph. D. 503 pages. 8vo. Cloth. $3.00.

**The American Workman.** By E. LEVASSEUR (translation). 540 pages. 8vo. Cloth. $3.00.

**Herbert B. Adams: A Memorial Volume.** 232 pages. 8vo. Cloth.

**A History of Slavery in Virginia.** By J. C. BALLAGH, Ph. D. 160 pages. 8vo. Cloth. $1.50.

The set of nineteen (regular) series is now offered, uniformly bound in cloth, for library use, for $57.00, and including subscription to the current (twentieth) series, for $60.00. The nineteen series, with eighteen extra volumes, will be sold for $76.50.

## THE ALBERT SHAW LECTURES ON DIPLOMATIC HISTORY.

**The Diplomatic Relations of the United States and Spanish America.** By J. H. LATANE, Ph. D. 294 pages. 12mo. Cloth. $1.50.

**The Diplomatic History of the Southern Confederacy.** By J. M. CALLAHAN, Ph. D. 304 pages. 12mo. Cloth. $1.50.

THE JOHNS HOPKINS PRESS, BALTIMORE, MARYLAND.